THE EGO DEATH OF AMERICA

Academics and Politicians destroy the identity of America
as fake social & news media champion disinformation.

SHAWN MORROW, M.ED., PH.D.

Stop telling immigrants to assimilate and start helping them participate.

World Economic Forum

Completion of this manuscript has taken years. Years not from research, but by what happened to me in academia.

I've been homeless, picking strawberries, potatoes, and stocking shelves at Pat's General Store to help feed my family at five years old in Elkton, Ohio after steel mills crash of late 70s in Pennsylvania. I've cleaned up classrooms after teachers, students, and had to serve coffee at the school's administration office while I was a janitor to make ends meet. I've had the honor to run into burning homes to extinguish structure fires, chase after criminals while wanted, armed, and dangerous; only to be physically and mental assaulted by senior faculty members at the university after serving many years as alumni and teaching.

Before you read ahead, I want you to know this manuscript might challenge your ideas and beliefs.

That is not my intent.

I want to be as honest as I can bringing readers along as I have my own life experiences while seeking ways I can help society. I've had the honor serving American communities as a First Responder, Fire Fighter, Jailer, 911 Dispatcher, Juvenile Cadet Leader, Sheriff's Deputy, Police Officer, Public School Teacher, and PhD Professor.

My goals are to continue researching gathering health and knowledge of potential solutions.

We The People cannot let America go.

Public virtue is a must. Go vote.

Contents

Part I
Low Voter Turnout Among Hispanics in Texas

Part II
Social and News Media's Affect on Law Enforcement

THE EGO DEATH OF AMERICA

Prologue

August 5th, 2017, 8:52pm

Growing up I used to say, "watch out world I'm going to be famous." Famous? My journey has twists, turns, among potholes defining and redefining me into who Dr. Morrow is today. In order to understand who I am, you must first forget the (average), usual human beings that go with the flow never to question anything! Not for me!

Always ask: WHY?

Always be the student, never give up, don't stop until your passion, Society is NOT here for you. You must work hard Research, Investigate, take personal responsibility, Develop Public Virtue helping others. These actions have lead me to greatness and they can help you. You have been Morrowed.

This knowledge will not be politically correct. Nor will the information be grammatically correct to my wife's horror. This knowledge comes from 40+ years of personal experiences of heartaches, homelessness, emergencies, some crazy, some unbelievable.

All of these stories have one thing in common, they ALL happened to me.

Believe what you will.

I pray and thank God every day. God has put me on this earth to help others I knew this since I was around 10 years old. Please sit back & open your minds.

Friday, August 11, 2017, at 10:20 PM

As a child, life was simple but we grappled financially. The basic Maslow's hierarchy of needs were not being met. Worry for food and shelter were always at the forefront. Toys, a bike, or hopes for Christmas were out of question. Both my parents worked hard trying to make ends meet after the steel mills crashed in the 1980s in Pennsylvania.

Millions of middle-class family were dealt a major blow losing their livelihood, housing, cars, and millions of us lost our generational wealth. State unemployment offices were not ready for the thousands of workers that were laid off.

At six years old, I was picking strawberries and potatoes for a local farmer who employed my family so we could work for food. Jim and his wife Pat, the owners at the general store, allowed me to stock the coolers and front shelves for a bologna sandwich with an RC cola to drink for lunch. Elkton, Ohio was a small blimp on the map as farming community with one stop sign and a general store called Pat's.

This type of life had me grow up a little fast, but I was ready to help. I loved running around out in nature by the river searching for hidden treasures in the wild. I've always felt natural to be out and about always looking for a purpose.

Each year, Elkton held a festival celebrating its heritage. The Native Americans from the Shawnee Tribe came out and participated. They taught me how to earn a Shawnee painting of the face by learning how to properly throw the axe.

My Grandfather, Pap Howard would come over and setup a tarp canopy for campsite while he fished. We could see him through our kitchen window, in our two-bedroom apartment above a taxidermist. My Pap Howard taught us how to make cornmeal bait to catch largemouth catfish. He would camp for days at a time. Sitting in his lawn chair, playing his acoustic guitar, singing old blues songs and tell stories. Elkton town's residents would stop by and listen.

"Shawn! Yes, Pap?"

"Go get me a six pack of Pabst Blue Ribbon from the general store."

"Okay, I'll be right back."

Pap taught us never give up. I watched him; even after heart attacks and cancer, he would fight a fish he hooked for what seemed like hours. Either the line broke, or he reeled the fish in. He did the same thing in life— from the stories my father and my uncle who was a bouncer a bar would tell us.

Listening to stories of adventures helps to pass the time, but telling stories breaks the ice in opening up a new course and meeting a new people. I enjoy learning details of events in history firsthand or close as possible to the action. As in martial arts, I do in learning and teaching, I want to help pass true linages forward.

As a child, after watching television shows on Egyptians, Roman Gladiators, or world wars. I pretended using G.I. Joes, or the little green soldiers acting out scenes I remembered from those stories. From eight to ten years old, I would write stories while my father sat inside a convenience store called Shot's #2 telling stories and writing poetry. Any chance I had playing with the kids in the neighborhood usually ended up being football or hide and seek, but I felt as if I didn't belong.

My family history consists barely surviving the steel mill crash while we lost the house, the car, and then having everything taken from us as we were forced to move in 1981. We were low-middle class and ended flat broke. We stood in food lines. Each of us held a box as people from the food drive would fill the box with foods such as cheese, cereal, bread. We would go from there to the welfare office and unemployment office. They qualified us for food stamps the kind that looked like fake money. We lived a short time at each new rent house— moving address to address as we continued not being able to pay for rent.

We had an old car that my parents were able to get somehow. My mom was driving and I was with her. We went to see my grandmother and, on the way back, the gas tank fell of the car leaving us stranded on the side of the road in the middle of nowhere. We walked a couple of miles to a residence to try to get help. They never opened the door and my mom sat down on the steps of the house crying and had wet herself. I didn't know what to do.

Peeling another onion layer, my father Tom is a Vietnam War veteran with a service connected zero disability head injury — with th onset of epileptic seizures with full black outs, cold sweats. He does a rebooting phase after he comes to. He would begin repeating his date of birth, social security number, and then states, my brothers' names, and date of births. He continues repeating it as he becomes alert. His head injury occurred in Fort Benning Georgia in 1967. My entire life my father has had Post Traumatic Stress Syndrome. In December of 2004, I did the research, built a case, and finally got him one hundred precent disability with the Veterans Administration.

My parents found out that friends in Elkton were moving to Texas where the economy was booming with oil. We sold what little things we had and moved from Elkton, Ohio driving 1,400 miles to Ozona, Texas in summer of 1984.

Our family of five moved, traveling across the United States as I slept in the back window of the 1976 faded blue Plymouth old four-door cop car. Once we made it to Ozona, we moved into a small two-bedroom house— 20ft x 30ft size. Our new house had rats flying out of the water cooler and we hit the ground struggling. I will later purchase this house as a single man trying to create stability for myself at the age of 21 for a payment of $194.18 a month, because I knew I could always make the money to pay for it.

Public School didn't help either. Lacking motivation stemmed from money for food and shelter continued as public-school teachers gave busy work to do. So yes, the basic schoolwork didn't help my energy and didn't maintain my attention. I was a low C student at times when I was bored. If the subject was interesting my grades would reflect it. I hardly studied. I was more worried about the roof over my head and if I would have something to eat at the end of the day.

Poverty followed with us for years.

My mom lost her eyesight —the beginning stages started when she was 39 years old. We had always struggled to make it, this just made it even harder to get by.

In 1989, my parents were told of better opportunities in Waxahachie, Texas at a Baptist children's home. That turned out to be a lie. We again were homeless. I watched the kids in the home that my aunt and uncle worked at get food, clothes, toys (many of them actually got two of everything—bikes, boom boxes, and G.I. Joes), and so much more. My parents bought me a candy bar for that year's Christmas.

My dad was able to find work at factory, then later as a maintenance man at the elementary school. That job paid very poorly —less than seven hundred dollars a month for a forty hour a week position. We moved into a paid weekly run-down hotel to have a roof over our heads. Twin bed, roof leaked, and we had bugs. My brother Mike and I slept on the floor and my parents in the bed. Things didn't get any better. We stayed in poverty but we were able to move to an apartment complex. From 1989 through 1994, we struggled— survived by welfare, parents worked several jobs to try to keep us afloat. My mom did end up getting disability but it was far less than she made working.

In 1994, my parents decided to move again but back to Ozona this time. I was a senior at Waxahachie High School and I wanted to graduate before moving again. I needed to figure out what was next. I was left at the apartment until the rent ran out. Then, I was supposed to go live with my brother Mike, but that fell through due to his partner Alice, that woman hated me. And my brothers and their families still do as of September 2024.

I found myself homeless again in after graduation in May of 1994. I lived out of my 1971 Chevelle for a couple weeks until friends of mine who I had babysat for offered me their couch, and that was iffy since they smoked a lot of weed. I didn't want to get into trouble. My best friend, Shay allowed me to crash a few times at his sisters' on their living room floor.

In August of 1994, I decided I was not cut out for street living. I moved back to Ozona, Texas to live with my parents at the Country Club Apartments. I went to work for NATGAS with my oldest brother reading gas meters and installing new gas lines.

Then, in September, I would realize years later that this moved saved my life more ways than one.

I worked for the Country Club Bar as a bartender. I found myself living in the Crockett Apartments on HUD rental assistance program as a single guy. I was working at the gas company part time and bar tending part time at the Country Club Bar.

I began attending at the Ozona Fire Department grass fires that September. Ozona is located in Crockett County, Texas which consists of three thousand square miles of rocky pasture. The department had a hard time to find enough people to serve and I found myself attending as many calls as I could. I got a lot of on the job training during that fire season.

I enjoyed being on a different side of the situations based on it was already occurring naturally since I was ten-years-old. Growing up, I had a natural ability to being at the right place and the time emergency event would occur. The department sent me to fire school at Texas A&M Fire School to study Fire Fighting I, II, III, IV and Pump Operations. I also attended Methods of Teaching at Texas A&M Fire School after winning a grant to attend. That's until I broke the mold of being a volunteer only by traveling to Lubbock Texas to be a fireman at the old Reese Air Force Base. I agreed to work my first contract in September 1997. My love of all things community service and firefighting began to pay off and when I went to Lubbock Texas. Soon enough, I found the company Pro-Tec Fire Department was not paying the firemen the right amount of money that was promised. I was extremely disappointed, but needed the work to survive.

Soon, Sheriff Shane Fenton called me up asking if I wanted to join the Crockett County Sheriff's Office. I moved back to Ozona in March 1998, but this time but it was to work for Law Enforcement.

I was making $1,050.00 a month. Working 48 hours a week. Sheriff Fenton had brought me into law enforcement to begin a program working with inmates as a jailer out in the community, watching them do yard work as I mowed to help assist the county road department. (At the time I wrote this section, I got word he passed. ~Prayers to Sheriff Shane Fenton's family.~)

I also worked inside the Sheriff's as dispatcher. I enjoyed my work and took pride in how hard I worked; even though the Chief Jailer would tell you otherwise— another lesson learned that you can't please everyone.

I attended training as offered and shadowed officers by riding along. Then, in December of 1999, right before our first child was born, I found myself at another juncture in life this time challenging my ethics and morals. I was accused of deleting the file folders on the main frame by the drug interdiction officer. The officer could not locate his personal file folder and began clicking and moving folders around, even deleting files in his panic. It's important to note the office had just moved from typewriters to computers in the department— and there was NO training other than, "Don't mess it up," by the Chief Deputy. The Sheriff didn't believe I didn't delete the files and asked for my resignation. This one hurt. Hurt my pride from being accused and losing a job that demands honesty. Here we went again, the familiar ground of instability for my family.

A friend, Ruben gave me a job lead as a Cadet Leader for the Sheffield Juvenile Boot Camp in Sheffield, Texas. We celebrated a Happy New Year, as I started my new job. I had to travel 42 miles each way—mostly on the interstate 10 to get to the boot camp. The juvenile boot camp cadet leader position was to monitor the inside of a classroom that had been converted into dorm rooms with 180 juveniles ages 11 to 18 years old all from all over Texas. Quickly, I found out that screaming and taunting cadets was status quo. I would not partake in that, and understood that the atmosphere was not for me.

I found work as a maintenance man at Ozona High School and in August of 2001, I began the Concho Valley's Texas Basic Peace Officer Academy. The classes were couple nights a week and most Saturdays for the next nine months. We studied thirty-two subjects— over seven hundred hours of training— to serve as Texas law enforcement officer. We did two weeks physical training mirroring Tae Bo for self-defense. After nine months, I passed the two hundred and eighty question test.

My first position was a Reserve Deputy in Tom Green County Texas where San Angelo is located. After a short stent there, a friend from the academy reached out with a job lead in Winters, Texas to work for Chief Brian McGonagill. As I signed up, he was on the way out to finish a PhD in physics. The city was great get your start at if you were old school, that's whole other book.

Each time I attended training, I felt like I should be the one up front teaching the class. By the time I had started law enforcement I had already attended three to four thousand hours of training in fire safety and first aid. I thought about bringing my expertise in firefighting and law enforcement together as a fire investigator, but I wanted more.

ONE

Leveling Up

In June 2002, I signed up to Howard College for an associate's in criminal justice. In eleven months, I finished their two-year degree with a 3.94 GPA. I finally found my love of learning to be fed in a way I could excel. At graduation, I told them I would be back one day to teach.

I started courses at Angelo State University majoring in criminal justice and psychology in 2003. Three years later, I graduated with honors with a different vision. I understood that America has a lack educators who have actually worked for the entities they are teaching about. At times, there is a disconnect in subject matters that need a set of skills built throughout the knowledge being taught. I knew that higher education must revolutionize teaching reality using educators from the streets with the ability to transform experiences in a curriculums and I wanted to be a part of it.

Therefore, I realized that if I am going to be educating others, I needed to learn the best ways to send a message. So, I signed up for University of North Texas Masters in Secondary Education, Gifted Talented, Social Studies Texas Teacher Certification, and a Certification in Curriculum Development. At the same time, I began teaching government and AP History at San Angelo ISD in January 2008. And in the fall semester of 2010, I started teaching political science at Howard College. Dr. Casey Jones was a certified teacher monitor for students in the internship portion of the degree and UNT hired him to supervise me teaching government. Dr. Jones told me that he was fascinated and rejuvenated in teaching after watching me teach the twelfth graders how American government works.

Wanting even more, I signed up for PhD courses at Walden University in 2009 to study Law in Public Policy and Administration Terrorism, Mediation, and Peace. Dr. Casey Jones asked me to teach Political Science in the Spring of 2011 at Angelo State. And in March 2014, I was hired full-time to teach Security Studies and Criminal Justice. I stayed busy teaching four to seven courses and advising more than three hundred students, while helping in every way that I could each semester.

I quickly learned that Academia was just as full of corruption, hatred, and abuse as I has experienced during my time working for local, state, and federal governments.

TWO

Academic Toxicity

In 2015, the exhaustion kicked in from PhD burnout and teaching in a department that took pride in the high levels of academic toxicity.

I spent five years working to complete my dissertation while Walden University had revolving door of five chairs and committee members for my dissertation. On the surface you might think , "Oh five years no big deal, or so what?" You are correct. To the normal human individual that time would not have been considered too long, but I am not normal at least from what my therapist has told me.

The Walden dissertation phase put cracks into my full potential at serving Angelo State University with making my life extremely difficult by not allowing me to finish my degree in order to fully qualify for the positions being offered over and over to me.

Being a professor inside the classroom challenging students to open their minds one issue at a time is my dream job. Yet, every time I told my dissertation chairs, they quickly found a reason to not let me pass in time to accept the positions, over and over again, to the point it became mental abuse. I had accomplished getting into the classroom, teaching students foundations of the political and criminal systems of America. My life became even more difficult as colleagues at ASU were abusing me mentally and physically as I was trying to make a living for my family while working what was supposed to be the dream job for me.

During the third residency at George Brown Convention Center in Houston Texas, our fellow PhD Cohort from Nigeria presented his oral presentation of his dissertation up in front of the class. After presenting and going through his power point, his chair of committee awarded him his PhD. "Wow this is amazing." I thought as we both started at the same time, taking classes together, and yet only after six months in the program he finished. I was excited one of us was allowed to finish in record time, but I couldn't figure out why I wasn't being allowed to move forward with my PhD work.

I had already lost three career promotions at Angelo State University. Those career promotions would have been from part time instructor to full time tenured assistant professor, as well as more than a $2o, 000 raise, and most of all it would have provided family stability, insurance, and benefits like I'd only dreamed of.

During the dissertation phase at Walden, I attended four

required residencies in person. I absolutely loved attending each one. Chicago and Houston were the two locations I attended. I was able to meet other PhD students from all over the world. The PhD conferences allowed my eyes to be opened to the predatory practices of the university as students from Congo, Nigeria, Honduras, Brazil, and Australia all received their PhD confirmations with a presentation at the conference after completing just six months of PhD work at the university. I couldn't help but question why I was in my fourth year of PhD phase as I watched this process happen in front of my face.

In summer of 2015, I was told by my chair of my department at ASU, Dr. Jones, either finish the dissertation or goodbye. Now, you're probably thinking GET the dang dissertation done. Yes, again you are correct. I have hours of audio recording from the chair, co-chair, and committee members of ASU; along with Walden's deans, provost, and ombudsman all making excuses. I had re-written the dissertation four complete times and once in 24 hours after being told by Walden chair to hire a specific editing company by my PhD chair so that I could "pass" — only to have that company steal and resell my original dissertation paper. Once, I was instructed to rewrite my dissertation due to it sounding too much like a text book and it need to be dumbed down— that month I rewrote my dissertation 15 times in 30 days—not once being allowed to use track changes to allow for accountability on the chair's behalf. I have the audio proof if you want to hear it.

I have a law enforcement officer mentality with an Inspector Gadget and Pink Panther each at of my sides while Batman is in the sky way of thinking. This is me experiencing the onset of ADD as well as a taste of anxiety that allows my mind to be hyperfocused. By that time in the dissertation process, I had saved EVERYTHING dealing with Walden and my mental and physical health was showing it.

The problem with the evidence I collected was we knew who's fault and failures at WALDEN University it was, BUT there was/is no recourse. NONE to get them to treat student (me) right. I went one hundred and fifty-eight thousand dollars plus in student loan debt.

Intimidating them with a lawyer, showing some of the audio evidence to department head, ombudsman, deans, president, social media, nothing seemed to work. Each time, I would act and ask for solutions to finish and received little to nothing.

The deans picked another chair, and another chair, and another chair, and more members. I explained to them my career at my alumni university was doomed unless I completed my PhD.

The Walden University Dean contacted my Chair of the department at Angelo State University Dr. Casey Jones to explain what the situation was. Both said I was being mistreated.

In the end, it mattered naught, I lost the promotions and would end up being terminated after 10 years of service.

As of December of 2019, my contract was bought out through May 2020 from Angelo State University due to health reasons, per the Provost.

THREE

Change is Good They Say

Poverty had once again graced us.

Twenty-three years married and we still had to time to fall flat, as the money runs dry. After a decade of teaching at the university enjoying teaching the students every day even though I was abused. But once again we found ourselves out of money to live by. I was no longer able to provide for my family.

I had built a small network of potential university to teach at, but in Spring 2020 the country was shut down due to a worldwide virus.I filed to have my retirement released in order to face the current crisis. We moved to Hutto, Texas to be closer to Austin the potential university employment. I wasn't about to stop doing what I love.

But this time felt different. I had an underlying health issue that was taking a toll on my body. For years, I had been back and forth to more than a dozen doctors with severe back pain and other symptoms, sometimes unable to walk. Crawling to the bathroom to try to go was almost hopeless. I already had C6-C7 neck fusion in 2006, but since 2001 I continued to have inflammation in the joints, pain, numbness, and nerve twitching in my muscles.

April 2023, I was approved for Medicare at 47 years old after having another cervical neck fusion at C5-C6 in March 2022. Medically, I have ankylosis spondylitis of the spine, herniated L1-2, L2-3, T7-8, and arthritis of the S1 joints as well. Severe inflammation has damaged my left shoulder, both hips, and have peripheral neuropathy— in the legs mostly.

No Tenure

My problem was never my ability to teach or my attendance to work. I had made arrangements for appointments and procedures around weekends and the days I didn't teach. Faculty in my department used my condition against me. The actions within the department and the administration, as well as faculty government did nothing to help even investigate or bring my issues to a fair hearing. Once I did not get the proper response from the chair after being assaulted by a senior faculty member for retaliation that just happened to be in front of my young child and wife. The chair did nothing. I cried during our meeting as I realized I had been assaulted. I had been a cop, I used to taking a statement had not ever thought I would be having to give one at work, much less that it would be ignored. Please, do not put up with this type of abuse.

I was mistreated by the academic systems of Walden University and Angelo State University with mental and physical assaults. I worked as police officer and didn't get mistreated as bad as I as did by colleagues in academia who were jealous and wanted to take my degree and career from being too honest. Once I found out the level of corruption and abuse each are doing the abuse only increased.

Now, I see even more happening in the news—with the Harvard president having to step down, and other universities coming out with major plagiarism, misappropriations of funding, and physical abuse.

The Angelo State University president did step down two months after I was let go for health reason and they bought my contract out instead of promoting my earned tenured as the data shows.

My morals, beliefs, and values have been and will be challenged, but I am not giving up on educating others finding the truth asking the right questions using scientific methodologies.

Each time these major life situations break me to tears. As the years pass on, I find my body is slowing down rapidly.

Please don't squash the birdie.

FOUR

America is Undergoing a Cultural War

Turning toward an American lens we can see a national trend of the woke society that I had been a victim to. San Angelo Texas is located in west Texas in what is called the Concho Valley.

The Concho Valley area serves 13 counties with San Angelo as the largest city at over hundred and ten thousand in population. Angelo State University serves a little over ten thousand students with most of them now on-line.

Education should not be a one size fits all mindset.

America's fake social and news media platforms are manipulating narratives for corrupt politicians who are selling America to highest bidder. As an individual who was evicted by academia Spring of 2020, I had a front row seat. After teaching a decade of political science, security studies, and criminal justice. I found myself not fitting in with those degrading education.

My continued research focuses on marginalized people and amplify their voices.

We must participate in our polity for our needs to be met. I've served our communities as a Reese Airforce Base Fire Fighter, Juvenile Boot Camp Cadet Leader, Sheriff's Dispatcher/Jailer/Deputy, City Police Officer, Public High School Social Studies Teacher, & Assistant Professor of Political Science, Security Studies, & Criminal Justice to help create positive social change.

Education is key for people's voices to be heard.

Serving as a Peace Officer in the State of Texas was an honor. My experiences from academy to the street taught me more than any academic education could. The level of politics that hinder enforcing the law was shocking. My experience in emergency services varied from a county more than 3,000 square miles but only a population with 4,500 to a city that serviced 110,000 people in population. Demographics of each have similar issues to the United States of America with increased crime rates, corruption, drug smuggling, drug dealing, and manufacturing along with human trafficking.

Therefore, I knew, being a law enforcement officer would not provide the level of authority I was seeking to create positive social change. Societal issues such as the opioid epidemic, legalization of marijuana federally, corruption in politics, human trafficking, and building communication communities to fight back on crimes must be made throughout our system governing the people.

Thus, I attended University of North Texas and attained a Masters in Secondary Education, Gifted & Talented, Curriculum Development Specializations as well as a Texas Social Studies Teacher Certificate. I began teaching social studies at public school then community college. As I focused on a PhD degree at Walden University in Public Policy and Administration Law, Terrorism, Mediation, and Peace with research focus on marginalized voters; I was asked to join the Political Science Department at a university.

I realized people do not know the truth. Remember, we cannot say all, yet America's public-school systems on average are underfunded, understaffed, undereducated, and not always up to date. American politicians are lying to get into office and they continually lie to the American people to stay there. Social and news media platforms indoctrinate billions of users across the world by reporting and posting miss or dis-information on current events. Falsified information is posted online at 70% of the time compared to facts. An article from Peter Dizikes at MIT found humans responsible for the majority of misleading information (Dizikes, 2018).

Educating people of all backgrounds requires enhanced knowledge on the different ways people learn. Education should not be a one size fits all mindset. As professors, we need more than just a content specialty. Educators need skills to distribute learning materials and instructions. My Masters in Secondary Education, Gifted, Talented, and Curriculum Writing provides me tools to effectively teach others to learn research and investigative skills to find their truths on whatever topics they choose.

FIVE

American Society 2024

The American political environment in 2024 is alarming. Trust in the current White House Administration elected in 2020 is at an all-time low. Failures in the Biden Administration in leadership with open borders, Ukraine War, lockdowns, and economics are bringing America closer to World War three. Public anger across The United States is malingering as inflation is costing the American voting demographics more to have basic needs. The people are waking up to political lies, negative economics and failed foreign policies from outliers in podcasts like the Joe Rogan Experience. Joe Rogan conducts long format interviews up to four hours discussing current events that have uncovered lies and facts on major topics, such as, medicines used during the lockdowns that the social and news media outlets publish fictitious stories to hide the truth.

Falsified reports, post, and repost are magnified throughout social and news media triggering more negativity, hate, and violence (Zu & Hatuka, 2023). Attacks on politicians and law enforcement using lies, slander, character smashing, and physical violence from threats to murder have all increased in recent years (Wolfe & Nix, 2016). These increases in attacks and violence damages voter turnout in future elections from a lack of trust and dangerous conditions.

The chaos and distrust increase as voters decide to vote or not to vote. "The marginalization of any group of people in American should not occur in today's society (Morrow, 2015)."

SIX

American Fake News, High Crimes, & Low Voting

The purpose of this research was to extend further into the effects of low civic engagement and participation, social and news media's fake news has on law enforcement. Societies are heavily influenced by what they listen to and observe in their own environment.

Prior research has focused on the nature of Hispanic voter's as well as why participation levels are so low among this group (Morrow, 2015). Distrust in the government, gaps in education, cultural preferences, and social and news media contribute toward lower voter participation as well as a negativity toward law enforcement. As distrust in government increases society becomes increasingly more dangerous causing a vicious cycle of de-policing and criminal behavior.

The Presidential Election of 2020 furthered the distrust in government officials with lock downs, manipulation of data, fake social and news media caused more chaos. The continued posting of fake media threatens law enforcement officers causing them to be ambushed, assassinated, and political officials targeted with violence at their homes (Morrow, 2019). Americans who use social media to get news find more falsifying facts of events and know less about politics (Mitchell, Jurkowitz, Oliphant, & Shearer, 2021). Social media giants like Facebook, X (formerly Twitter), Instagram, and Google are using their platforms to censor American's freedom of speech.

Each Presidential election brings about a new level of toxicity. Social and news media outlets are censoring events to influence their users through ads, posts, or banning of them (Anderson, 2024). The global internet also provides openings for other countries to meddle in America's election process. Countries use social media platforms and search engines manipulating the information presented to the American people.

Could potential voters be affected accessing misinformation within these platforms? Could the social and news media's false information cause harm to other people such as law enforcement officers? Could individuals falsify information through the use of the internet and corrupt an election?

PART I
Low Voter Turnout Among Hispanics in Texas

ONE

Introduction

Civic engagement is critical for ensuring that a citizen's voice is heard. Chapa and De La Rosa (2004) argued that participation in the polity by Hispanics is very low in general, and mobilization in the southwest Texas communities is particularly lacking.

There are 41,574 Hispanics in Tom Green County, and of those, only 2,430 voted in the elections in 2012 (Tom Green County, 2011). Previous chapters have demonstrated the lack of civic engagement and the probable role of marginalization in this lack of participation in Tom Green County, Texas. While past researchers have looked at nation- wide characteristics relating to the lack of Hispanic participation in voting, there are few who have sought to explore the underlying reasons why the lower voter turnout still exists. Large-scale, quantitative studies have focused on population trends and the answers to limited survey questions related to voting. Relatively little work has explored the individual level perception beyond simple surveys. Hugo and Taylor state the 2012 elections show an increase in Hispanic voting, however, Tom Green County Hispanics voter turnout was far below national average (2012). Hispanic voter turnout is well below their 36% of the population in Tom Green County. By not actively participating in the political process the Hispanic community is not being properly represented by their elected officials. This perpetuates the pattern of marginalization and disenfranchisement that occurs within the group in the local community. A lack of participation leads to a lack of representation, which in turn leads to a perception that representatives ignore

Hispanic interests, reinforcing the idea that politics does not matter to the potential Hispanic voter.

This research has explored the individual-level perceptions of Hispanic voters in Tom Green County. The goal has been to understand the perceptions of civic engagement and voting in order to explain the lack of participation. While limited, this study sheds light on how the larger quantitative trends are reflected in individual perceptions. While the impact of the study is limited by the relatively small number of participants, it does demonstrate that the simple relationships derived from large-scale quantitative research miss important issues that emerge from these interviews. This study shows the importance of a deeper understanding of individual motivations if we are to design public policies and grassroots efforts to promote greater participation among Hispanic voters.

I have detailed the research questions that are the foundation of this study. I sought to understand why Hispanics are not participating in the polity in spite of the potential benefits to their community. As previously discussed in Chapter 2, Beaver and Chaiviano (2011) stated voters assimilate into their communities when they are both educated and knowledgeable.

The research question of this study was as follows:

1. What barriers keep Hispanics from being fully involved in voter participation? There were three overarching questions:
2. Does culture keep Hispanics from fully participating in the civic engagement?
3. What are the barriers to community involvement faced by the Hispanic population in Tom Green County, Texas?
4. What are the reasons behind low rates of registrations and low voter turnout among the voting age Hispanics population in Tom Green County, Texas?

To find the answers to these questions, I interviewed 20 participants who met the self-selection criteria for this study explained in Chapter 3. The interviews provided an opportunity for data collection related to individual perceptions of the conditions facing potential Hispanic voters in Tom Green County. Participants expressed their perceptions about the causes of low participation rates as well as the impact the lack of participation has on the Hispanic community in Tom Green

County. Chapter 4 includes sections related to setting, demographics, data collection and data analysis, evidence of trustworthiness, results, and a summary of the chapter.

Lack of Civic Engagement

The Hispanic population's lack of civic engagement resulting in low voter turnout was investigated in this study. Hispanics participate at much lower rates than other ethnic groups according to the current quantitative evidence. In the Literature Review, evidence evolved around issues of low voter participation using similar methodologies that conclude that eligible voters are deterred from the current electoral system. However, researchers have failed to answer why Hispanic voter turnout is low (Jacobson, 2001). I used critical race theory to describe and interpret the cultural or social group's patterns of behavior, customs, and ways of life and found ways to change it for the better (Crenshaw, 1995, pp. xiii-xiv).

In this study, I examined whether the responses in open-ended qualitative interviews match the findings of inductive empirical studies. The attempt to clarify theories derived from empirical research has clear support from the data. Research has been developed using a cultural lens to understand the phenomenon and the gap of knowledge in the literature that could be explored using a deductive approach (Patton, 2002).

Many citizens in Tom Green County in District 72 do not register to vote, and many of those who have registered do not participate by voting. State and federal benefits for business improvement, education, health maintenance, and public safety are contingent on numbers of registered voters and voter participation for electoral votes and the number of seats in both houses of Congress. When citizens do not vote in the scheduled local, state, and national elections, allocations of benefits are denied or decreased. Thus, lack of voter participation affects educational and financial opportunities. As noted in Chapter 1, Hispanics make up a significant portion of the population of voters, and their participation is much lower than their share of the population.

Not participating in the election process keeps the Hispanic population from being fully committed to and engaged in the political community. Lack of commitment to participating in the polity and voting correlates to policies and laws that affect the Hispanic population regarding personal liberties such as immigration, affordable healthcare, and education. When people or groups do not participate in voting, those not voting are letting other people and groups pass regulations and policies, and attention given to them because they spoke through voting.

TWO

Causes of Low Voter Turnout

Research for this study concerned Hispanic Americans in Tom Green County in Texas District 72. Hispanics in the county do not vote at rates comparable to other groups. This lack of participation is well documented from past elections (Tom Green County, 2011). The Hispanic population lacks involvement and political mobilization in Tom Green County. To understand this lack of participation in the polity, I wanted to discover the causes of the very low voter turnout. Lack of representation has had negative effects on the Hispanic population including marginalization, lack of representation in the political polity, and not being allowed to voice their identity. Therefore, Hispanics are receiving significantly less representation in the political realm than deserved.

To analyze the reasons behind this lack of participation, this study used an ethnographic approach. Interviews were used to collect data concerning individual perceptions of the lack of Hispanic voter participation. Interview questions asked the participants their feelings about civic engagement and attempted to draw out explanations for low Hispanic voter turnout. The qualitative ethnographic method allowed me to learn personal experiences from the participants experiencing the phenomenon in Tom Green County.

Research questions asked of the participants focused on information gathering pertaining to societal or racial barriers to voter participation in Tom Green County, Texas. Demographic information data were collected and included in the research results. In addition, questions asking to identify barriers or cultural distrust were asked.

Analyzing factors contributing to lack of Hispanic American voter participation and civic engagement in Tom Green County have provided me an in-depth perspective of the phenomena of why Hispanics believe that their group participates in voting at such low rates. More civic engagement by the Hispanic population using the information analyzed could provide the group with opportunities to create social change in their own community.

I review the literature and show a gap in knowledge of why Hispanic Americans in Tom Green County in Texas District 72 participate in low voter turnout. I also review the literature on how the Hispanics are being disenfranchised in Tom Green County (Battle & Pastrana, 2007).

I describe the critical race theory methodology that was used to conduct the research (Patton, 2002). The process of collecting data through interviews of Hispanic Americans is also explained.

Critical ethnography provided insight on the phenomenon of the nonvoting behavior of Hispanic Americans in Tom Green County in Texas District 72.

THREE

Marginalization of Hispanics

The marginalization of Hispanics is one the biggest challenges of Tom Green County, Texas, District 72. One of the most visible signs of marginalization is lack of civic engagement among the Hispanic population. During the presidential election of 2012, only 43.5% of all registered citizens participated in the vote (Texas Legislative Council, 2012). Hispanic voter turnout was extremely low at 16.9% even though they make up a significant portion of the population. This lack of participation is reflective of the national trend of low Hispanic voter turnout (Texas Legislative Council, 2012). The lack of voter participation by Hispanics keeps them from being a part of the polity and limits their access to the provision of government services. Marginalization affects state and federal benefits for business improvement, education, health maintenance, and public safety. These benefits are contingent on numbers of registered voters and voter participation.

When Hispanics do not vote in the scheduled local, state, and national elections, benefits are potentially denied or decreased. Thus, lack of voter participation affects educational and financial opportunities for members of the Hispanic community (Bonilla- Silva & Glover, 2006). Voting is not merely choosing a favorite candidate; voting gives the voter a voice in the issues, concerns, and needs of the community. Lack of civic engagement by Hispanic community members causes underrepresentation of their voice. Overrepresentation of non-Hispanic voters results in a lack of attention to the needs of Hispanics in passing laws. Voters in elections determine allocation for benefits including which persons and entities receive benefits, and where the funds flow in society. Local, state, and federal governments listen to the voters to determine who will receive benefits and where to allocate funds. By voting, citizens can improve their own well-being and that of the community.

Lack of voter participation leads to a lop-sided allocation of benefits beginning a cycle of thinking that voting does not have benefits. Citizens who do not vote still have expectations that the government shall supply equal benefits to them, but politicians do not pay attention to their needs. Hispanics are being underserved, which puts them in a vicious circle. Lack of civic engagement also affects local, state, federal taxes, and supplemental funds creating a downward cycle that is impelled by lack of voter participation, thereby marginalizing Hispanics further. When federal and state funding to the county declines, citizens' employment opportunities or wage rates, educational levels, personal health and safety are endangered. Citizen's ability to be prepared to vote and travel to the polls is further decreased, perpetuating the downward cycle (Dutwin et al., 2005).

Therefore, Tom Green County, Texas, District 72 faces serious problems arising from the lack of citizen participation. Lack of Hispanic citizen participation has worsened since the year 2000 (Texas Legislative Council, 2012). This trend shows the importance to Tom Green County of understanding the underlying causes of this reduced participation. Discovering the causes of non-participation can help the county remediate the problem. To understand voting trends in the district, I examined census data and four types of election data—national, state, district, and county—to determine which groups of citizens are not voting.

Voting Demographics 2000-2012 State Population

Texas had a population of 26,403,743 citizens in 2012, which was a 26% increase from the 2000 U.S. Census (U.S. Bureau of the Census, 2012). Texas has experienced steady population growth since the year 2000 and has faced changes in political representation for the state at the national level. Table 1 shows the relevant population data and its national political impact. Since the year 2000, total population of the state has grown by nearly 6 million people (U.S. Bureau of the Census, 2012). As a result, Texas gained a significant increase in representation of the State of Texas in federal politics. The state boosted its share in the House of Representatives by eight seats over the last two reapportionment cycles, resulting in significantly increased power in the House (2000 and 2010). As Electoral College representation is based largely on House of Representatives seats, this has led to a similar increase in the power of Texas in the election of the president (U.S. Bureau of the Census, 2012).

FOUR

Texas Demographics

Comparing official racial categories from the United States Census is challenging. Redefinition of the term Hispanic occurs commonly from census to census. The Hispanic ethnic/race group is treated differently than other groups (Dutwin et al., 2005). Census categories will be discussed further in Chapter 2. For the purpose of this study, all ethnicities and race categories are listed as defined by the U.S. Census Bureau. These race categories are listed as follows: White, Black, African, Negro, American Indian, Alaska Indian, Asian Indian, Chinese, Filipino, Other Asian, Japanese, Korean, Vietnamese, Native Hawaiian, Guamanian, Chamorro, Samoan, and Other Pacific Islander. After all of these, Hispanics are still only counted by origin/ethnicity, not race (U.S. Bureau of the Census, 2012).

In 2010, Texas had a total population of 25,145,561 in which Hispanic Americans were 37.6% or 9,460,921 of the population

(Texas Legislative Council, 2010 Census, Red 600, p. 7). Texas had a voter age population (VAP) of about 18.28 million, of which Hispanics formed the largest minority group (33.6%; U.S. Bureau of the Census, 2012).

In the state midterm and gubernatorial 2012 elections, the lowest voter turnouts comparing VAP occurred in the western and southern districts of Texas along the border.

The lower voter turnout compared to VAP districts included Districts 80 following the border to District 35 of Texas to Mexico.

These districts include counties of El Paso, Pecos, Val Verde, Dimmit, Webb, Starr, Hidalgo, and Cameron (see Figure 1; Texas Legislative Council, 2012).

I was particularly interested in District 72 in the southwest of the state. District 72 consists of counties of Coke, Concho, Glasscock, Howard, Irion, Reagan, Runnels, Sterling, and Tom Green (see Figure 2).

6

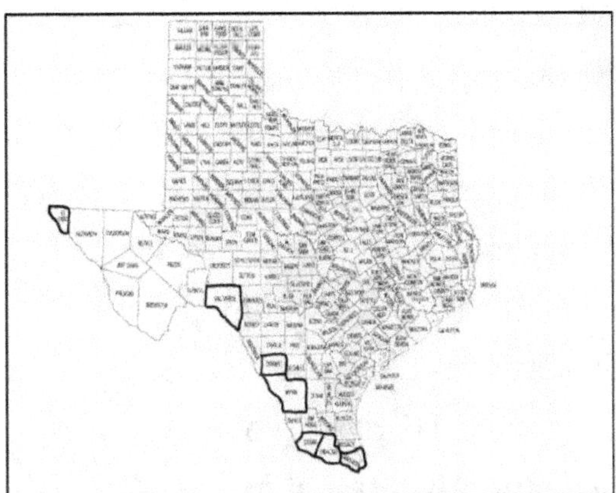

Figure 3. Map of southwestern Texas counties with low voter turnout in the 2012-midterm state elections. Adapted from U.S. Bureau of the Census. (2011). *Voting and registration in the election of November 2010: Tables* (p. 20). Retrieved from http://72.census.gov

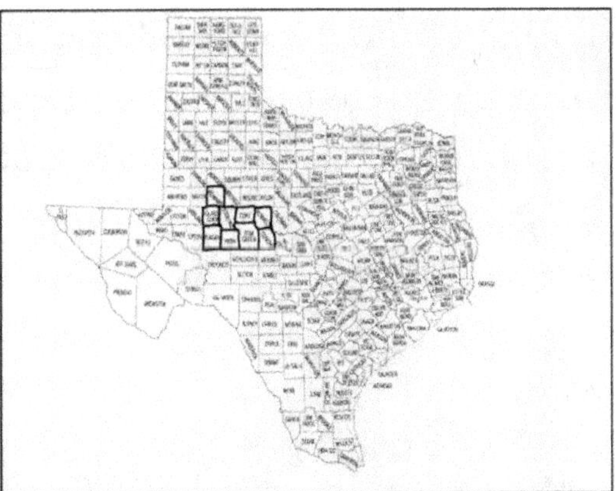

Figure 4. Map of the nine counties of Texas District 72 with lower Hispanic voter age population turnout. Adapted from U.S. Bureau of the Census. (2011). Voting and registration in the election of November 2010: Tables (p. 20). Retrieved from http://72.census.gov

Texas District 72 Demographics

IN 2010, the Texas District 72 had a population of 170,479 (Texas Legislative Council, 2010 Census, Red 119, p. 2). Total Hispanic VAP, based on the Spanish surname voter registration (SSVR), was 22,011 (24.1%) as listed with the U.S. Bureau of the Census (2011). Therefore, if turn out (TO) /voter registration (VR) was only 59.4% of registered voters, one can estimate that the number of Hispanic TO/VAP would be decreased by 45.5%, and Hispanic TO/VR would decrease by 59.4% indicating a TO of only 13,075 registered Hispanic voters or 14% of the 24.1% who had registered, as shown in Table 2. The TO/VAP was only 41.5%, indicating a larger Hispanic population along with low voter turnout. Furthermore, if the estimated available Hispanic VAP was 28,698, but only an estimated 13,075 Hispanic persons voted, only an estimated 5% of the Hispanic VAP voted.

Table 2

Texas District 72 Population Totals With Hispanic Surname Voter Registration and Estimated Turnout

	Population 2010		VAP 2010		Total VR 2012		Total TO 2012	
Ethnicity	Number	%	Number	%	Number	%	Number	%
Hispanic American	61,883	36.3	42,239	32.3	21,991	24.1	8,784	16.2
Total	170,479	100	130,771	76.7	91,253	69.8	54,277	59.4

Note. Ethnic groups other than Hispanic were not available on this census page. VAP = voter age population, VR = voter registration, TO = turnout. From Population, VR, and TO Analysis with County

Subtotals for District 72, Red 119, 2010 Census, County Population Analysis, House Districts – PlanH358, 2012 General Election, by Texas Legislative Council, June 27, 2013, p. 6.

In 2010, the Texas District 72 VAP was 130,771, and in 2012 registered voters consisted of 69.8% and voter turnout was 43.3% as listed with the U.S. Bureau of Census (2011). In this same election, Hispanic or Spanish Surname VAP was 32.3% or 42,239. Of those Spanish surnames, 24.1% or 21,991 registered and 16.2% or 8,784 turned out to vote (U.S. Bureau of the Census, 2012). The Hispanic voter turnout was extremely low compared to other groups.

Tom Green County Demographics

In 2000, Tom Green County in the southwestern part of Texas had a population of 104,010 people of which 65,508 were White Americans (63%), 4,757 were Black Americans (4.6%), and 31,946 were Hispanic Americans (30.7%; U.S. Bureau of the Census, 2012).

In 2010, Tom Green County had a population of 110,994 people of which 63,820 were White Americans (57.9%), 5,290 were Black Americans (4.8%), and 39,349 were Hispanic Americans (35.7%; U.S. Bureau of the Census, 2012).

In 2012, Tom Green County had a population of 113,281 people of which 64,117 were White Americans (56.6%), 5,210 were Black Americans (4.6%), and 41,574 were Hispanic Americans (36.7%; U.S. Bureau of the Census, 2012). See Table 3.

Districts – Plan H358, 2012 General Election, by Texas Legislative Council, June 27, 2013, p. 6.

County demographics--voting age population, registered voters, and turnout

In order to understand the lack of voter turnout, I looked at the voting age population, registered voters, and who turns out to vote. In accordance with Texas state law, the state only collects Spanish surnames of those who registered and turnout to vote. Of the 2010 census 110,224 people recorded in the population in Table 4; 84,290 were in the VAP (Texas Legislative Council, 2010 Census, Red 600, p. 7). Of the VAP, Hispanic Americans were 31.5% or 26,516. However, of the 59,909 total registered voters, only 36,720 (61.3%) turned out to vote in the 2012 general election, giving a TO/VAP of only 43.6% (Texas Legislative Council, 2010 census, Red 236, p. 6). Furthermore, of the 26,516 Hispanic VAP, only 14,378 (24%) registered to vote, and only 2,430 (16.9%) voted, as shown in Table 4. Hispanic voter turnout is far less of a turnout compared to Whites and Blacks (Lopez & Taylor, 2009).

FIVE

Hispanic Americans Not Voting

Of the Hispanic population in Tom Green County, only 16.9% (2,430) voted in 2012 elections out of the 26,516 of Hispanic voting age in Tom Green County, Texas (U.S. Bureau of the Census, 2011). The Hispanic population lacks involvement and political mobilization in the communities in southwest Texas (Chapa & De La Rosa, 2004). The voting patterns and demographics on the Census Population Survey (U.S. Bureau of the Census, 2012) validate the low rate of participation of Hispanic Americans not only in Tom Green County but also across the country (Harrington & Liu, 2002). The data from the U.S. Census, redistricting office of Texas, Tom Green County Elections Office, and PEW Research all provide data comparing data of VAP, registered voters, and voter turnout comparing the lower turnout by Hispanics compared to those of Whites and Blacks (U.S. Bureau of the Census, 2012).

This lack of community involvement has become an increasingly critical issue in society. Pink (2009) demonstrated that declining levels of achievement and motivational characteristics in the population overall have become more serious issues in recent years and have remained unresolved. Policies by the federal government focus on welfare, immigration, and health care instead of assimilating the Hispanic population into the polity by promoting participation in civic life (Bonilla-Silva & Glover, 2006). Without assimilation into the polity, the Hispanic population fails to receive benefits that could improve its well-being (e.g., education and infrastructure).

Therefore, it is necessary to analyze the Hispanic population's involvement in the community to understand its voter mobilization characteristics that determine its level of participation in the political process (Dutwin et al., 2005). In analyzing the lack of political mobilization and its effects on the Hispanics of Tom Green County in southwest Texas, I wanted to discover motivations or lack thereof that have caused this very low rate of voter turnout.

The Hispanic community has played a significant role in the United States becoming a dominant power in the world (Lopez, 2008). However, Hispanics in Tom Green County participate at lower numbers than other groups in the electoral process. When Hispanics are not fully involved in the voting of their counties, they give up their voice in society. Without their voice, their needs are not articulated to political leaders. Without such articulation by voters, these needs are not addressed.

The United States has levels of governmental authority in which city, county, state, and federal governments share power in a complicated system of federalism. In this system, the dominance of one level of politics over the others has shifted overt time.

From the early 1900s until the 1930s and the Great Depression, Americans had a sense of government not being as involved in the everyday life of the individual as it is today.

Today, Americans want government to regulate and provide social benefits such as welfare, food stamps, and healthcare (Arias, Schauman, Eschbach, Sorlie, & Backlund, 2008). Murray (2009) showed that from 2008 to 2009, welfare from the federal government increased over 25%. Welfare has increased since the New Deal government regulation on individuals, including Hispanics; increasing government involvement in the lives of Americans into the entitlements the country has today (Arias et al., 2008).

Literature exists exhibiting marginalization and challenges for the Hispanics in the quantitative data collected in Chapter 2. However, an empirical study of Hispanic voting data fails to answer why they are participating in the voting process less than the other groups. Gaps and deficiencies exist in research on Hispanic lack of community engagement and assimilation into the polity, including low voter participation. Therefore, I was interested in the voting patterns regarding political process concerning Hispanics and the marginalization that prevents their representation in the polity. A literature review of Hispanic voting participation and mobilization shows Hispanics that their lack of voter participation results in severe harm in this community. If Hispanics are not participating by voting, politicians are ignoring them, and no one is looking out for their best interests. Hispanics need to articulate their desires and demands to their politicians via the ballot box.

Motivational characteristics (Dutwin et al., 2005) might also explain why the Hispanic population does not participate in the voting process. Not seeing the value in participating, low voter engagement exposes Hispanics to marginalization. The lack of voter participation in the Hispanic polity means that there is significantly less representation in the political realm than they deserve. Dutwin et al. (2005) and Pink (2009) discussed motivational topics in depth and explored why people become motivated. Two kinds of rewards contribute to motivation: extrinsic and intrinsic rewards. Hispanics need to participate in voting to make their needs heard at the ballot box. Further research on analyzing the voting mobilization and participation of the Hispanic population could provide insight into and understanding of this phenomenon (Dutwin et al., 2005).

Hispanics participate in voting at much lower rates than their counterparts. Marginalization results in Hispanics being underserved in terms of access to government services. This marginalization is disparaging for Hispanics because it prevents assimilation into the political polity.

SIX

Statement of the Problem

Hispanic Americans in Tom Green County are being marginalized within the polity. Hispanic Americans of voting age in Tom Green County, Texas, District 72 participate at much lower numbers than projected in the political community. When Hispanics are left out of the polity, adverse impacts occur. For instance, Hispanics have less access to public services. The lack of Hispanic assimilation into the polity should be addressed because of failures in social, economic, and educational areas (Pew Research Hispanic Trends Project, 2004). Previous research on Hispanic voter turnout has been quantitative and has identified trends in the population, but researchers have found little agreement on the motivations that drive such trends. Thus, I have conducted an ethnographic study to explore the motivations behind low Hispanic voter participation.

By exploring the motivations behind low voter turnout by

the Hispanic American voting age population, my investigation provided insights into the underlying barriers to participation. These insights can help design policies or programs to help remedy the situation. The United States is pluralist, and it is a fight to get any funding for any group or need. Battle and Pastrana (2007) have argued that the Hispanic population is growing, and their lack of participation will lead to marginalization of an increasing percentage of the population. This will affect federal funds if they do not fully participate in the election process. High birth rates and increasing population of Hispanics means that an entire generation will be underserved.

To address the lack of Hispanic voter participation, public administrators must know more about this phenomenon. The results of this critical ethnography will help public officials and researchers to understand why Hispanics are not fully participating in the community of Tom Green County. Based on this understanding, they will be able to design policies that can encourage greater Hispanic participation in the life of the polity.

SEVEN

Nature of the Study

Critical ethnographic methodology was employed using interviews as the primary data collection approach. I sought out the underlying evidence that explains why registered Hispanic American voters are not voting in the context of these competing empirical explanations. Hispanics in Tom Green County, Texas, District 72, are participating at lower numbers compared to other groups that vote. Interviews were recorded with a digital audio recorder and notes were taken. Data from the interview consisted of open-ended questions. The interviews with each participant were limited in time to 1 hour. I interviewed 20 Hispanic American participants who stated they are nonvoting.

In the interviews, I asked Hispanic Americans about voter participation in Tom Green County, District 72. Interview questions asked how the interviewees felt about civic engagement, and I attempted to draw out explanations that were relevant to existing empirical explanations for low Hispanic voter turnout. I selected this method to observe the phenomenon through the cultural lens of critical race theory (Patton, 2002). Critical race theory is defined by Crenshaw (1995) as a movement of scholars who focus their work challenging the way race and racial power are represented in American society.

Critical race theory has allowed researchers to study the role of race and inequality in society. Johnson and Onwuegbuzie (2004) wrote about research paradigms and how researchers working with human subjects respect the representative approaches of social groups and their reporting of participation levels. Research using the critical ethnographic approach depends on human participation and respect of their opinions. The critical ethnographic approach allowed me to ask the Hispanic participants interview questions to discover why participation in voting is lower than expected. While studying this phenomenon, Creswell (2007) stated that the ethnographic method could be used to explore why groups and individuals are politically motivated within the environment in which they live. Furthermore, Hatch (2002) argued that qualitative research can be used to understand behaviors and participation levels of people. Therefore, the qualitative ethnographic method allowed me to learn personal experiences of the group experiencing the phenomenon (Creswell, 2007). Hatch (2002) stated that the researcher who uses qualitative research could create social or political change by providing the policy makers information by using the data collected to find the weaknesses in Hispanic voting patterns. Hence, the application of critical race theory would illuminate the marginalization of the Hispanics. The construction of specific theories in specific cases highlights the mechanisms of marginalization. I assembled theories supporting the critical race theory method in order to create possible change in marginalization for this group.

Creating opportunities for social or political change led me to develop an approach that is grounded in critical race theory to help shape the polity's involvement in voting.

Participants from the local Hispanic community were nonvoters. This study is an ethnography based on a purposive sample of members of the Hispanic community. I conducted the data collection analysis in a manner consistent with professional standards for data security and the protection of participants, locking the data in a file cabinet and protecting the electronic media with a password. Collected data from the interviews were coded, classified, and scrutinized. I interpreted the views of the participants without adding or altering the data retrieved (Hatch 2002). Then, I offered suggestions for action to promote social change.

EIGHT

Research Questions

In this study, I explored causes for lack of voter participation by Hispanics in Tom Green County, Texas. The focus of this study was informed by the asking of open- ended questions during the interview process. The questions invited information about societal or racial barriers to voter participation in San Angelo, Tom Green County, Texas. The following questions were used to address what is happening to Hispanics here in Tom Green County who lack voter participation:

Overarching questions:

1. What barriers keep Hispanics from being fully involved in voter participation? Sub questions:
2. Does culture keep Hispanics from fully participating in the civic engagement?

3. What are the barriers to community involvement faced by the Hispanic population in Tom Green County, Texas?

4. What are the reasons behind low rates of registration and low voter turnout among the voting age Hispanic population in Tom Green County, Texas?

NINE

Purpose Statement

Ethnography using critical race theory was used to determine the reasons that Hispanic Americans in Tom Green County, Texas, District 72 are voting in numbers that are low relative to other groups. Hatch (2002) stated, "Critical ethnography describes part of the culture from the point of view of cultural insider" (p. 21). Creswell (2007) defined critical ethnography as having the characteristics "where authors advocate the emancipation groups, politically minded individuals who seek, through their research, to speak out against inequality and domination" (p. 70). Through this critical ethnographic study, I analyzed the factors contributing to the lack of Hispanic American voter participation and civic engagement in Tom Green County. I identified barriers that affect Hispanic American voting behavior. Furthermore, when I discovered the barriers to Hispanic American voting, the barriers were recorded in detail and analyzed in Chapter 4 with recommendations for remediation made in Chapter 5.

Possible causes of lack of voter mobilization are government regulations, culture, education, and the ability to speak and read the English language. Barriers might cause lack of Hispanic assimilation, increasing their failures in social, economic, and educational areas (Pew Research Hispanic Trends Project, 2004). Researching the impact of the growing government regulation on the population in the United States, the issues for Hispanics were characteristics of voting, health care, public education, and immigration. Another possible barrier is voter motivation. Pink (2009), Maslow and Frager (1987), and Harrington and Liu (2002) conducted research on the topic of motivation. Extrinsic and intrinsic rewards and incentives help to determine and describe the motivation (Harrington & Liu, 2002). Research on what motivates (or fails to motivate) the Hispanic population provided insight into the reasons for their lack of community and political participation.

Throughout the literature review, in Chapter 2, I have examined other authors' studies to determine whether they have already identified possible reasons why Hispanic Americans do not vote. I have incorporated this prior research into the design of the interview instrument in order to identify possible causes of the lack of voting. The survey of the literature in Chapter 2 demonstrates that there are multiple competing empirical explanations in the existing quantitative research. In this study, I explored the actual conditions that contributed to the lack of participation and lack of civic engagement (Battle & Pastrana, 2007).

TEN

Theoretical Framework

Ethnographic qualitative research needs a theoretical framework for the researcher to place the findings in the context. In this ethnographic study, the interview questions focused on culture, relationships, and societal views of the lack of Hispanic voter participation in Tom Green County. LeCompte and Priessle (1994) engaged in ethnographic qualitative research structured to include smaller groups of interviewees in naturalistic locations. Therefore, I completed these interviews in a natural location because it made the respondents more likely to respond truthfully. Moreover, research from Clarke (2010) demonstrated that determining disenfranchisement was complex.

Clarke explained that research of marginalization requires participant observation or interviews to understand how the actions of individuals make up the marginalization of a group, in this case the Hispanics of Tom Green County. Due to the classification of Hispanics, the disenfranchisement was occurring in their identification and their position in the polity. Clarke stated that ethnography distinguishes the powerful and the powerless in an ethical manner; thus, ethnography studies are done in order to protect the disenfranchised. In order to engage in social action for the marginalized, I looked at the root of the issues while maintaining quality of the research.

The ethnographic approach was required to generate a more holistic picture of the position of the subject. Ethnography permits a study in much greater depth than other methods. Ethnographic qualitative research incorporates critical race theory because it is a study of individuals race, culture, and location. Price (2009) stated that legal scholars and practicing lawyers developed critical race theory. Developing critical race theory was a response to the eroding of concern of racial equality after the huge push in the 1960s.

These scholars saw a need that needed to be filled legally in order to provide individuals legal equality and worked together to create the critical race theory.

Creswell (2007) wrote that critical race theory was a theoretical lens through which the researcher could conduct a qualitative study of racism to determine whether a group has been disenfranchised. Price (2010) expanded on Creswell's theories by explaining critical race theory's main introduction to the United States was to "question the outcomes of Civil Rights era legislation" (p. 150). Price theorized that critical race theory was needed because of the erosion of racial equality that was gained in the 1960s. Critical race theory has been applied to the study of legislation or data to identify the problematic issues in Hispanic culture that contributed to low voter participation.

The ethnographic method provided the alternative in-depth perspective of phenomena through questioning participants within the culture. Ethnography was appropriate when the existing quantitative methods and theories did not fully explain the issue because the research emphasizes on the cause rather than testing therefore, the focus was directed at "why" the phenomenon of the underlying structure has occurred rather than the numbers of lack of participation (Lecompte & Priessle, 1994). Qualitative data allowed the interview questions to ask why Hispanics participate in the polity less than others. Thus, an ethnographic study applying critical race theory was an appropriate approach in this case.

The phenomenon of nonvoting Hispanic Americans requires more than simple quantitative analysis. Using the ethnographic method grounded in critical race theory, I expected to obtain a complete and holistic view of the phenomenon (Creswell, 2007). I looked at the social construction while engaging the ethnographic method. Therefore, I chose an ethnographic method applying critical race theory as a theoretical lens with which to examine the phenomenon of nonvoting Hispanic Americans, describing the results of the study of the phenomenon to fill the gap in the literature.

ELEVEN

Scope of Study

Interviews included in the study were Hispanic participants from Tom Green County, Texas District 72. Participants were selected from the Hispanic community and completed short interviews.

Interview questions were listed on a single page in both English and Spanish. The interview consisted of 12 questions. I recorded the interviews with an audio recording device. I interviewed until saturation was reached, the expected number of subjects required was 20. The participants were volunteers and were able to leave or stop the survey questionnaire at any time during the interview. I protected the anonymity of all of the participants by not publishing their names or their addresses.

One of the questions included in the interview was a question about the use of public services provided to the community (e.g., public schools, the U.S. Post Office, and emergency services), as the use of public services may have contributed to civic engagement. Hispanics need representation for how tax money is allocated for the use of services in the community or are remunerated for those services through government taxes. Barriers to Hispanic voting and community participation have been identified to increase their community involvement and voice.

TWELVE

Assumptions

Researchers are aware of the assumptions that may be true but cannot be verified. Researchers must not make postulations about an unbiased reality that exists apart from the individual when conducting phenomenological research (Mertens, 2005). Mertens (2005) explained the importance of understanding the phenomenological experience from the viewpoint of the participant. In order to investigate why Hispanics are not participating in civic engagement and have a low voter turnout, I asked the individuals who experience the phenomenon.

Creswell (2007) listed the five philosophical assumptions that provided guidance in qualitative research: axiological, epistemological, methodological, ontological, and rhetorical. Using ontology in ethnographic methodology provides realities that are defined and interpreted by the culture-sharing group (Creswell, 2007). Keeping in mind that various realities may be true from an individual's perspective, I have also assumed that participants provided truthful responses during the interviews.

I have assumed that the interviewees were willing to cooperate in completing the interview. It is also assumed that gaining access to Hispanics who do not participate in civic activities or the voting process in Tom Green County would not be a problem.

Furthermore, it was assumed that the nonvoting Hispanics were willing to allow me to interview them for my research.

THIRTEEN

Delimitations

Participants were selected only from Tom Green County, Texas, District 72. Only Hispanics were asked to participate (Texas Legislative Council, 2012). The results of the research could be generalizable to (a) registered Hispanic American voters residing in Texas District 72, (b) registered Hispanic American voters, and (c) and nonregistered Hispanic American citizens.

FOURTEEN

Limitations

Although the study was about Hispanic Americans, interviewing all Hispanic Americans living in Tom Green County in Texas District 72 was not possible; therefore, data were collected from a sample of participants from the Hispanic Americans living in Tom Green County in Texas District 72. Hispanics were self-identified. Another limitation of this study was the process of completing the interview.

Participants might generalize their views or might not understand the questions. Communication gaps involved in the study might create a problem for the participants and me.

FIFTEEN

Significance of the Study

Despite the increase in numbers of Hispanic Americans in Texas District 72, not all of them were voting (Chapa & De La Rosa, 2004). Hispanic Americans are negatively affected in Texas District 72 through lack of political representation. Voting patterns from elections and U.S. Bureau of the Census (2012) indicated voting must increase in order to provide representation commensurate with their proportion of the population in political life.

Past researchers using quantitative methods have identified two broad theoretical schools, rational public choice theory and cultural explanations. However, these broad theoretical schools and the research that go along with them did not allow viewing the problem in sufficient depth in order design effective policies. Lack of civic engagement has become an increasingly critical issue in education, and it affects all students and staff in local schools (Igalens & Roussel, 1999). Analyzing the factors that contribute to voter turnout and participation of Hispanic Americans might provide them a voice.

Government agencies, nonprofits, businesses, and political candidates would benefit from research on the barriers to Hispanic community involvement. More civic engagement by the Hispanic population would bring greater ownership in their communities, increasing their political representation and voice. The present study on Hispanic civic engagement was important because of the current lack of Hispanic representation and voice. Hispanics could not be accurately represented if they did not participate fully in the community and political process. Hispanic community leaders needed help informing and motivating the Hispanic people to be involved in the polity (Arias et al., 2008). Hispanic Americans are one of the fastest growing populations in America (Chapa & De La Rosa, 2004). Therefore, using critical ethnography, I explored the underlying causes of lower rates of voting among Hispanics.

SIXTEEN

Literature Review

Hispanics do not participate in political life in levels that are commensurate with their percentage of the population. I also observed this phenomenon in Tom Green County. In the following literature review, I discuss this lack of participation and competing explanations for it. The empirical literature points to multiple directions without agreeing on why Hispanics are not voting. With only statistical studies, it was not possible to determine which competing theory of rational public choice theory and cultural explanations was correct. In this dissertation, I sought to explain the causal mechanisms of what leaves Hispanics out of the political process. The stage was set for that discussion in this literature review.

In Tom Green County, Texas in the 2012 general election, only 2,430 of the 26,516 of the Hispanics of voting age turned out (Texas Legislative Council, 2014). Compared to other groups, Hispanics had a very low turnout (Chapa & De La Rosa, 2004). However, research on Hispanic voting did not portray a consensus why this occurs. The lack of civic engagement has become an increasingly critical issue. Bonilla- Silva and Glover (2006) asserted that the Hispanic's lack of civic engagement could be from a historical marginalization or not seeing the value of voter mobilization. In this study, I investigated the phenomenon of why Hispanics are not participating in the polity of Tom Green County.

Literature Search

In the literature review, I followed standard methodological practices for researching Hispanic voting literature. The literature investigation concentrated on autonomous Hispanic voter participation as well as Hispanic voting behavior patterns. My enquiry encompassed articles published in journals that ranged from the 1970s to the present. The empirical studies I found focused on the numerical data of what prevents the Hispanics from voting and the patterns that could be traced geographically, I wanted to find the why of what prevents the Hispanics from participating in the polity. Organized research has provided an understanding of barriers and the lack of Hispanic voter participation.

The main databases used were Walden University Library and Google Scholar.

The keywords searched included Hispanics, Hispanic voting, voting, presidential elections, general election, voting rights, voting demographics, Hispanic behavior patterns, and voting research. In each search conducted, I looked for relevant articles that correlated to the lack of or barriers to Hispanic voting.

Past Theories and Empirical Studies

To understand the lack of Hispanic voter participation in Tom Green County, Texas, I synthesized research on this topic. The standard approach in researching voter participation or behavior is quantitative methodology. Quantitative research analyzes the relationship between and observed phenomenon such as voting and a range of explanatory variables. Quantitative research finds support for a hypothesis using quantitative data and predictive models. This research offers explanations, but quantitative methodology does not allow for distinction between them to find if one of them is correct or if it is a combination of both, that are correct (Creswell, 2007).

Quantitative method has tended to be numerical research that is about correlation and helps to see the why behind the correlation.

In reviewing the literature, it was clear there are multiple competing explanations, as discussed in Chapter 1, which are supported by empirical research. While there has been research done in both the quantitative and qualitative methods, the gap remained in terms of why Hispanics vote at a much lower rate than expected. In this research, I illuminate the problems that are prohibiting the Hispanic participation from voting in Tom

Green County. My research helps fill the gap in the literature that emerged from an inability to differentiate. My research also helps illustrate the experiences that quantitative research cannot illuminate because numerical data did not show why Hispanics vote less than others in Tom Green County, only that this lack of civil engagement has occurred.

Voter mobilization could be researched in a number of ways. The two main theories that are prominent now are the rational public choice theory and cultural explanations. Researchers who focused on rational choice conventionally measure participation in voting as a conditional cost theory that occurred through social networks (Rolfe, 2012). Teixeira (1987) explained that in the 1950s, researchers predominantly used voter participation theories using the quantitative, rational choice method. A classic example was the "calculus of voting" to be considered one's benefit costs associated with voting (Downs, 1957). Teixeira furthered the notion of the cost-benefit theory but added that it was a transaction with each step participating in the political process of voting.

Teixeira stated, "Voting is not a zero-cost activity; the cost of registering, finding out where the polling place is and taking the time and effort to travel to it on Election Day are tangible nonzero ones" (p. 5).

Santoro and Segura (2011) used measures of classic assimilation collected through a national survey to analyze empirical data on the likelihood of Hispanics being marginalized in politics. Theories of political participation and assimilation are used by Sanchez (2006) to identify generational status among Mexican Americans participating in the polity. These studies go into great depth to explain how Hispanics should assimilate and mobilize into voter participation but fail to identify the problems or offer solutions.

Santoro and Segura stated that there was little research on ethnic political activity that was more than descriptive.

Additional researchers have explored cultural explanations and have offered a variety of additional areas of concerns. Dutwin et al. (2005) stated that psychological theories in voting could be determined by the level of motivation to participate.

Moreover, Pink (2009) argued that psychological motivation could be a determining factor in why people do not act. Again, these theories give quantitative calculations of characteristics of those who vote or not, they tell certain behaviors correlated with certain principles, but they do not allow comparison of one group of factors against another such as rational choice theory.

Quantitative researchers used the United States Census data and the CPS to gather data to test hypotheses regarding the role of demographics in voter participation, but demographic data could not provide a full explanation (Logan, Darrah, & Oh, 2012).

These demographics indicated low socioeconomic positions and lower citizenship rates among others to be a characteristic to low voter turnout, but researchers have been asked to clarify why turnout was low (Logan et al., 2012).

Empirical research has indicated that when researchers looked at the populations as a whole, two competing schools of theory were present. While limited to the single county, this has provided a depth that was not possible in the large N quantitative studies. Large-scale quantitative surveys have failed to clarify the gaps in research by not fully explaining the phenomena of lack of voter mobilization. Quantitative surveys have not answered why Hispanic voters are not participating in the polity. In this study, I seek to answer why Hispanics do not participate in the polity in Tom Green County and to interpret the additional research of other counties in Texas. Interviews might give insight into the causes of low voter participation in Tom Green County (Creswell, 2007). The interviews might also reflect what Hispanics in the county feel by asking the meaning, structure, and essence of their marginalization (Mertens, 2005). Interviewing individuals rather than collecting numerical data while applying critical rate theory allowed me to hear from the Hispanics who did not participate in voting.

Instituting a qualitative research design such as an ethnographic study involved going into the community and culture where the phenomenon has occurred. I went into the community where the phenomenon was occurring in order to find answers to why low voter participation occurs, and I collected data that could be used in larger demographical areas in future research.

An ethnographic study describes and interprets the patterns of behavior, customs, and ways of life of the Hispanic community in Tom Green County (Creswell, 2007). The ethnographic method provided the alternative in-depth perspective of the phenomena through questioning the participants within the culture. Research working directly with the individuals involved in the phenomenon provided the best glimpse into their mindset. The use of critical race theory has provided a lens that focused on the phenomenon and the questions raised in the prior research such as low Hispanic voter turnout. Creswell (2007) stated critical theory could help explain this phenomenon that occurred in the world. The ethnography method was applicable when the existing quantitative methods and theories did not solve the drawback of low voter turnout among the Hispanics in Tom Green County in the western part of Texas.

Critical race theory has helped understand the lens in which people approached the issue. Price (2010) suggested that in order to find racial differences that have been normalized to the point of invisibility, these differences must be rendered visible. Making Hispanics aware of their own marginalization could lead to their participation in the voting process and therefore improve their levels of civic engagement. Understanding the social structure and experience of marginalization while researching low voter turnout allowed my research to be more informative. When dealing with a population who has been historically marginalized and left out of membership of the polity, it was important to see the issues from their perspective. One of the key elements was understanding what it means to be Hispanic.

Defining Who Is Hispanic

It would be impossible to discuss Hispanic voter participation without addressing being Hispanic in the United States. Unlike being another race (i.e., Black), Hispanic is an identity that is sometimes considered racial and other times considered ethnic (Hugo & Gonzalez-Barrera, 2012). Furthermore, the government has changed what Hispanic means over time. Talking about Hispanic voter identity has been fluid and not well defined, and this has led to obstacles for Hispanics who want to participate in the polity.

Before considering the concept of measuring the phenomenon of the Hispanic voter turnout, I asked, "Who qualifies as Hispanic?" In the decennial census, the Hispanic category became an ethnicity because of the U.S. Bureau of the Census (2012) and politics of 1970s (Jones & Correa, 2001). The U.S. Census Bureau stated,

These standards generally reflect a social definition of race and ethnicity recognized in this country, and they do not conform to any biological, anthropological, or genetic criteria. There are two minimum categories for data on ethnicity: "Hispanic or Latino" and "Not Hispanic or Latino." The concept of race reflects self-identification by people according to the race or races with which they most closely identify (U.S. Census, 2014).

This statement from the census demonstrated how Hispanic identity was confused when included in the census. Consequently, the vague and confusing options for self-identification given to Hispanics prevent them from properly completing the census. This marginalized the Hispanic population from polity because of the inability to properly self-identify due to the confusion between race and ethnicity (Harrington & Liu, 2002). As a result, Hispanics not completing the U.S. Census form properly led to underreported numbers. Therefore, Hispanics are cut out of the benefits that could be received from being part of the polity, adding to their marginalization.

In this historical context, the Hispanic item was not included in the census. A "color or race" item included in the 1970 census, which included the options of Indian (American), White, Negro or Black, Japanese, Chinese, Filipino, Hawaiian, Korean, and Other (Battle & Pastrana, 2007). The identifier Hispanic was left out until the 1980 Census but only included as an ethnicity, not a race (Hugo & Gonzalez-Barrera, 2012). Therefore, Hispanics were excluded from even checking a box on the census for their race, further marginalizing the Hispanic community.

The relevance and necessity of including race on the decennial census called into question in the 1960s led to the serious consideration of the removal of racial identifiers for the 1970 census. However, in the midst of the Civil Rights Movement of the 1960s, minorities (including Hispanics) gained leverage in public policy through such vehicles as the Voting Rights Act (1965), which banned racially discriminatory impediments to voting (Beaver & Chaviano, 2011).

To be accurately counted, Mexican American advocacy groups demanded a self- identification item on the 1970 census and insisted that the surname method greatly underestimated the size of the Hispanic population. The U.S. Bureau of the Census (2012) rejected the inclusion of a direct Hispanic identifier because of the lack of time available for testing and printing of millions of surveys that had already occurred. The White House then intervened, leading to the appearance of a Hispanic ethnic identifier on the 5% long-form sample of the census (Battle & Pastrana, 2007).

The Passel-Word quantitative surname method was created and developed for the 1980 Census, using the premise that last names of Hispanic sounding origin identify persons as being Hispanic when they live in a similar geographic location as other Hispanics (U.S. Bureau of Census, 2012). The U.S. Bureau of Census (2012) stated that one approach comprises of matching the respondents' surnames to a list of common Hispanic surnames. The list was created using highly and nonhighly Hispanic geographical locations and using mathematical equations to project that might or might not be a Hispanic Census filer (U.S. Bureau of Census, 2012). Texas adopted a similar method of counting Spanish surnames into law in 1990 and is still used today (Texas Legislative Council, 2012).

In a society where racial options only include White, Black, Asian, and some form of Native American or Pacific Islander, many ethnic Hispanics find their race not represented and subsequently identify as Other (Igalens & Roussel, 1999). When choosing, 40% of Hispanics have filled in "some other race" on surveys (Arias et al., 2008). Indeed, most would select a Hispanic race if given the opportunity to do so.

The struggle for recognition is also a problem for Hispanics in political participation. It reflects an ongoing struggle for identification as a distinct group with a clear identity comparable to that of other racial groups in the United States. Struggles that began during the Civil Rights movement caused them to not feel welcome in politics, thereby creating a generational shift of rejection. Marginalization that began then has continued for the Hispanics in the polity. The federal government's denial of the Hispanic identity has marginalized them in such a way that defeats the Hispanics involvement in the polity.

The U.S. government did not provide Hispanics a clear identity on the census equivalent with other groups identified such as White, Black, Native American, or Asian (Battle & Pastrana, 2007). A combination of undercounting the Hispanics in the census and decisions by the officials in the government to marginalize the population leads to stripping Hispanics of proper voice.

Hispanic Becomes an Ethnicity (not a Race)

Hispanics continue to experience marginalization in the collection of census data. For 5% of the census survey long forms, the questionnaire included many items after the race item, "this person's origin or descent," with the options of Mexican, Puerto Rican, Cuban, Central or South American, Other Spanish, and None. The 2000 census used neither "origin" nor "descent" to gather data on the Hispanic population. It asked; "Is this person Spanish/Hispanic or Latino?" which differentiated the personal identity from familial ancestry (Bonilla-Silva & Glover, 2006).

The category of (Hispanic) ethnicity was amplified due to the increase in that population in the United States. National Council of La Raza maintains support of the identifiers that increase Hispanic assimilation (Stevens & Bishin, 2011). In the Hispanic population, the categories identifying race and ethnicity are unclear, leaving more questions than answers. Over 40% of the Hispanics who do not understand how to identify themselves on the census choose "other" (Arias et al., 2008). In a society where racial options include only White, Black, Asian, and some form of Native American or Pacific Islander, many ethnic Hispanics find their race not represented and subsequently identify as "other".

Hispanic population cannot assimilate when they are not

given an identity within the polity. The U.S. Census among other federal, state, and local administrations failed to properly categorize the Hispanics as their own group. Current data from the U.S. Census has listed Hispanics under whites when searching demographics within the state (U.S. Bureau of the Census, 2012). Marginalization of the Hispanic population could be a barrier to voter mobilization. Research of low voter turnout investigates potential barriers causing the phenomenon by the Hispanic population in Tom Green County, Texas.

Hispanic (Origin or Descent): The Political and Historical Context

History of the identification embedded in each generation of a Spanish-speaking population was inevitably tied to the political context (Valencia, 2005). At all times, political interests involved creating a non-White population identified (whether Mexican or Spanish surnames) and counted. Through the 1920s to current day, the American government has worked to identify other race and ethnicities on the census form while still marginalizing the Hispanics.

Historical context of the 1920s was particularly sensitive to foreigners and immigration, as the American government was undergoing adjustment in the wake of World War I. European migration was limited, prompting the need to reach out to Mexican workers (Jones & Correa, 2001). In 1930, the "Mexican" category made its (first and final) appearance as a race in the American census.

Mexican Americans and the Mexican government opposed having Mexican as a racial category, demanding it removed from the racial options on the census (Bonilla- Silva and Glover, 2006). The Great Depression and massive deportations shadowed this event. A major factor in eliminating the "Mexican" category stemmed from the many rights that were only available to "Whites," not the least of which was the right to become a citizen.

Aside from the 1930 Mexican racial category, no items were included on the census that could directly measure any Hispanic population until 1970. Indirect measures of a Hispanic population were found in the 1940 "persons of Spanish mother tongue" item as well as the 1950 and 1960 "persons of Spanish surname" item (Bonilla-Silva, 2004). Relevance and necessity of including race on the Decennial Census were called into question in the 1960s, leading to the serious consideration of the removal of racial identifiers for the 1970 census. However, in the midst of the Civil Rights Movements of the 1960s, minorities gained flexibility in public policy through such vehicles as the Voting Rights Act (1965), which banned racial discriminatory impediments to voting.

Now, proliferating forms of federal aid became contingent upon population size and proof of discrimination (Beaver and Chaviano, 2011). A demonstration of past discrimination against the Hispanic population on the U.S. Census documents exists. Other groups were identified in the U.S. Census by race whereas Hispanics were counted by Spanish-surnames (U.S. Bureau of the Census (2012). Examining the data one could say the

Hispanic population suffered discriminatory interactions dealing with race within the polity when identified as white. Patton states, what gave critical race theory its name was that it seeks not just to study and understand society but rather to critique and change society (2002).

Importance of Hispanic Voters and Hispanic Voter Turnout

Hispanics have become the fastest growing population of voters in America (Passel, D'Vera, & Lopez, 2012). In the 2000 and 2004 presidential elections, George W. Bush, a Spanish-speaking candidate from Texas was able to split the votes more evenly resulting in a win. In the presidential election of 2012, Republican candidate Mitt Romney failed to reach the Hispanic population, whereas the Barack Obama campaign used an executive order to temporary stop deportations of certain illegal immigrants. Hispanic population in the 2012 presidential election voted 71% for Democratic incumbent candidate President Barack Obama, costing Mitt Romney the election (Hugo & Taylor, 2012).

If Hispanic political participation were to increase to full potential, would they vote one way or will their votes cause a more competitive electoral landscape of Texas? The potential of the Hispanic's mobilizing and the ramifications of that, it was impossible for us to predict. While Hispanic population was growing their rate of low voter turnout was continuing.

Hispanics have the potential of becoming the largest voting bloc in the United States (Hugo & Taylor, 2012). Political research has been conducted to look at the characteristics of registered nonvoters through quantitative methods, researching candidates' campaigns, but not discovering "why" Hispanics do not vote. If they vote at all—Hispanics vote typically for the Democratic candidates. (Battle & Pastrana, 2007) The Republican Party has not done enough to win over the Hispanic community on issues of healthcare, immigration, and voting rights (Hugo & Taylor, 2012). Political parties that attract the Hispanic vote would most likely be the winner of future elections. Clear information was unavailable about the effect on the political landscape if Hispanics change their voter turnout participation.

Political parties and candidates that campaign to the needs of the Hispanic vote could change the way Hispanics communicate their identity, while increasing the chances of winning the election. Hispanics are underrepresented; however, assimilation into the polity could affect the elections. Hispanic's lack voter turnout compared to the population of those who are eligible to vote was low (Hugo & Taylor, 2012). Increasing the Hispanic group's civic engagement and lessening their marginalization would be a product of increased voter turnout.

NINETEEN

Hispanic Demographics and Barriers to Vote

Immigration continues as a dominant issue for population growth in the United States (Beaver & Chaviano, 2011). Although, European immigrants dominated early population growth in America in the early 1900s, Central and South American Spanish- speaking immigrants are arriving in the United States at the highest rate today (Gerson, 2012). Mexican nationals comprised the bulk of the immigrants who entered into the United States (Valencia, 2005). The 2010 American census stated that the Hispanic population was the fastest growing demographic group in America; however, recent worldwide demographic shifts are caused by Hispanics moving away from their "traditional homelands" to opportunities in northern America (Beaver & Chaviano, 2011). In this portion of the literature review, I investigated the immigration patterns of the Hispanic population during the 20th century, which led to the present-day demographics of Hispanic populations (Gerson, 2012).

The United States Congress introduced firm visa policies for immigrants to enter the country in the 1924 National Origins Act. (Battle & Pastrana, 2007). Immigrants without a proper visa could be charged with a crime of a misdemeanor and deported. If the immigrant were to repeat the crime, that immigrant would be charged with a felony and possibly imprisoned up to 2 years (Gerson, 2012). American lawmakers in Congress believed that Hispanics would have difficulties assimilating into American communities thereby treating them different and changing their path to acclimatization. Critical race theory turns on the idea there was something unique about how a racial group sees itself (Mertens, 2005). In this case it was not that Hispanics saw themselves as criminals, but that the larger society constructed a concept of the "illegal" that included anyone who appeared Hispanic. This occurred in the society, not just in politics. This label created an unjust name or classification for Hispanics that entered the country illegally as being a criminal act, pushing them out of the polity. The combination of an assumption of problematic assimilation with the criminal status creates a marginalized other that is outside of society both by virtue of culture/race and by virtue of being criminal. The resulting image could be perceived (and was by many Hispanics) as equating Hispanic identity with the "illegal" who was excluded from society for being criminal.

Hispanic populations with Spanish surnames are calculated separately in California, Texas, Arizona, New Mexico, and

Nevada. Gathering demographic data on Hispanics did not account for the fact that many of them did not have Spanish surnames. Many of the Hispanic population lived elsewhere in the United States (Beaver & Chaviano, 2011). However, the 1960 census used the same measures again to calculate the data for Hispanics as they had in 1950. Researchers of the census were provided comparisons for the Hispanic population for the first time in American history (Antunes & Gaitz, 1975). Census techniques of calculating this population underestimated the numbers of Hispanic persons (Liang, 1994). Leaders from Hispanic organizations insisted on reforms in collecting data. Census data calculations are used to determine the funding given to federal, state, local agencies, and other programs benefit Hispanics. The U.S. Bureau of the Census (2012) still had issues regarding whether to classify Hispanics as a race and how to identify them (Erlach, 2000).

Mexico aided the majority of the Hispanic population who were Mexican Americans in the United States. Although disenfranchised, Mexican Americans did not want to be categorized as a race. Census officials struggled with this issue, and then asked three questions (Antunes & Gaitz, 1975):

1. For all other nationalities apart from an ethnic self-identification, should the category of Hispanic be used to determine identification?
2. What would be the relationship between racial questions and ethnic if they fill in Hispanic?

3. What was the validity of the use of Hispanic as an identification item?

The 1970 census reformed its tactics toward Hispanics (Antunes & Gaitz, 1975). In contrast with the 1950 and 1960 censuses, the 1970 census surveyed the entire United States for Hispanics. The census questionnaire gave American citizens the option of self- identification (Battle & Pastrana, 2007). Categories on the census originated with persons of Spanish origin; citizens would decide from categories, including Mexican descent, Puerto Rican, Central and South American, Cuban, and other Spanish. However, as with the 1950 and 1960 censuses, the census again simply counted the Spanish surnames in the same five states. After the 1970 census, Hispanics still had difficulties with being disenfranchised (Gerson, 2012).

Texas Congress passed a law in 1990, concerning collecting data on Hispanics, using Spanish surnames to determine voting age, a registered voter, and voter turnout populations. Monitoring voting patterns of people with Spanish surnames was the lawmaker's goal. Texas implemented this law to decrease the marginalization of Hispanics and their low voter turnout. Studies of Hispanic voting patterns could reveal the social structure of their polity and find ways to benefit their identity and race (Texas Legislative Council, 2012).

Legal Barriers

Discrimination hinders the Hispanic population, and that prevents participation in the American political process (Jones & Correa, 2001). However, the voting experience of Hispanics is often equated to that of the Black population (Gerson, 2012). Hispanics encountered obstacles such as White-only candidates or English-only ballots. Black and Hispanic populations are both disenfranchised politically by legal barriers (Dutwin et al., 2005). The 1965 Civil Rights Act was passed by United State Congress to make discrimination toward minorities against the law and reforming political discrimination at the polls (Battle & Pastrana, 2007). The U.S. Supreme Court and Congress both set the path of the passage of the laws against racial discrimination. In Reynolds v. Sims (1964),

the U.S. Supreme Court declared some state laws that discriminated against minorities and their capacity to vote were unconstitutional (Del Pilar & Udasco, 2004).

Political Mobilization Efforts

The Voting Rights Act (1965) eradicated many legal barriers to Hispanic participation in the political process. However, voting participation rates among Hispanics continue to be marginalized. Hispanic coalition building in the grassroots level in the polity takes place at a lower frequency than that for other groups. Nonpartisanship by the two major political parties at federal and state levels weakens the coalition building for Hispanics. At the national level, the two-party system creates supremacy of special interest politics reinforcing to Hispanics that their votes did not matter (Harrington & Liu, 2002). Rodolfo and Cortina (2007) gave quantitative evidence that Hispanic Americans have high poverty rates, residential dislodgment, and higher educational dropout rates. Political theory showed that individuals with higher socioeconomic income status were more likely to participate in political activities than those of lower socioeconomic income status (Gerson, 2012). Jones and Correa (2001) attributed this correlation to numerous factors. Factors of correlation included: (a) greater political opportunities afforded to persons of high social status, (b) greater political resources of those same persons, (c) more thorough acculturation of such persons into the values and techniques of democratic participation, and (d) the tendency of both formal and informal rules of participation to favor the upper-class lifestyle.

In general, Lopez (2011) argued that national political parties are being degraded by the acceptance of special interest groups and lobbyists working for their own agendas. Political factions have been created to further self-advantageous programs and policies, guided by the wealthy divisions of society marginalizing the Hispanic population. Battle and Pastrana (2007) suggested that the lower socioeconomic status of Hispanics made it difficult for them to compete with the wealthy when seeking representation in the political organization. Competition pushes national parties to try to attract as many factions as possible; to gain enough support to win national elections. Political parties' candidates running for office tend to focus on long-term agendas and accomplishments in terms of office held by the politicians. Persons of lower socioeconomic status focused on short-term welfare goals such as food, shelter, and paying bills (Passel, D'Vera, & Lopez, 2012). Therefore, Hispanics are disenfranchised from the political realm, leading to their lack of political participation (Beaver & Chaviano, 2011). The fact that national political parties ignored the Hispanic population cannot be attributed only to special interest groups. As the fastest growing minority population, inadequately assimilating into the political process defeated their representation. Potential political power from the Hispanic voting bloc could be directly tied to its level of assimilation and the culture brought into their communities (Gerson, 2012). Deardorff and Blumerman (2001) suggested that the lack of Hispanic political participation has been an opposition to White subjugation and supremacy (Dutwin et al., 2005). The Chicano Movement of the 1960s commanded young Hispanics to embrace their family heritage, questioning the white authority that controls the wealth of America (Arias et al., 2008). The Hispanics have shown interests in the past of wanting to participate in the polity, but still did not participate wholly due to the marginalization that was occurring.

The Hispanic Community Is Not Monolithic Generational Effects

Generations of Mexican Americans divided into first, second, and third generations are part of what makes the Hispanic community diverse. First subgroups that arrived directly from Mexico were labeled as first-generation immigrants. The issue was immigrants who arrived directly from Mexico might not be legal residents of the United States. Many of these immigrants lived closer to their native countries bringing traditional views of politics from Mexican. Immigrants typically lived within communities in El Paso, Texas, and East Los Angeles, California. Immigrants in this group could not vote because of negative legal status and American's see them as criminals. Immigrants belonging to this group also find themselves pulled between their native countries and now living in America. These communities focus on the bottom and basic level of Maslow's hierarchy of human needs (e.g., food, shelter, and clothing).

Until basic needs have been met, communities are less active politically (Valencia, 2005). Characteristics from these communities show low socioeconomic status, first-generation, non-English-speaking, and less educated Hispanics, therefore, less likely to be mobilized to vote (Chapa & De La Rosa, 2004).

Compared to other groups, second generation Mexican American communities are more active in political matters. Second generation Mexican Americans consisted of at least one parent naturally born. Individuals of this group were more likely to live further away from their native countries (Hugo & Taylor, 2012). This group represented 52% of the Hispanic population (Santoro, & Segura, 2011). The third generation of Hispanic Americans of Mexican origin remained attached to their Mexican heritage but participate more in local communities (Santoro & Segura, 2011).

Comparing the characteristics and changes caused by assimilation, researchers still could not find why the three generations of Hispanic Americans were not voting (Valencia, 2005). Communities of Hispanic Americans were somewhat different in political tendencies and regional makeup (Jones & Correa, 2001). Mostly, Cubans were situated in the Miami area, and most Puerto Ricans located in the New York City area, including New Jersey. Other communities include the Nicaraguan community located in the area of Orlando, Florida. Comparison also reveals that Hispanic and Latino or subgroups tended to vote for the Democratic Party when participating in voting (Dutwin et al., 2005). Mexican, Cuban, and Puerto Rican

Americans share generational patterns of assimilation into America society (Hugo & Gonzalez-Barrera, 2012).

Age of Hispanics

Hispanics were the fastest growing ethnic group (Hugo & Gonzalez-Barrera, 2012). In comparison with Blacks and Whites, however, Hispanic voters had an over 20% lower turnout in 2012. Blacks' voters in 2012 voted at 66.6%, and White voters voted at 64.1%. (Taylor, Gonzalez-Barrera, Passel, & Lopez, 2012) Among total Hispanic population, more than one in five voters belonged to voting age group of 18–29 years and one half belong to voting age group of 45–59 years. Fewer Hispanic voters belong to age group of 60 years and older (Beaver & Chaviano, 2011).

Hispanic's voter Aged 65 and older increased in 2012 from 56% to 59%. The trend of older voters participating more is noticed in the general population. Hispanic's Ages 18 to 29 had an increase of 36.9% in 2012, but voted less often (Lopez & Taylor, 2012).

Education and Income

The more educated a person becomes, the more likely they were to participate to vote (Taylor, Gonzalez-Barrera, Passel, & Lopez, 2012). More than 69% of the Hispanic populations were high school graduates, and 12% of the Hispanic voters have not completed high school. Voters with college degrees were the largest group at 70%.

Hispanics with some college in 2012 election were 54.2 %. Hispanics who graduated high school voted at 39.4%. The lowest voter turnouts among Hispanics were those who had less than high school education at 35.5% (Lopez & Taylor, 2012).

The average level of family income of the Hispanic voting population is $50,000 (Hugo & Gonzalez-Barrera, 2012). The Hispanic median income in 2010 was $37, 759. Hispanics who earned less than $50,000 voted at a rate of 82% for candidate Obama in 2012 (U.S. Bureau of the Census, 2012)

TWENTY-TWO

Motivation to Vote

Research on rational choice theory shows that in order to be motivated to vote, one must find the value to participate in civic engagement. Much of the literature focuses on whether or not to vote, based on the observed cost benefit of the vote. Characteristics of voters and non-voters of low economic status are more concerned about issues of meeting their fundamental needs such as health, food, and shelter, rather than who was running for political office. Persons who have met those basic needs and obtain a higher education are more likely to vote. Persons who have a college degree were prone to follow election information because of understanding the cost benefit gained by active voters. Higher educated people also have a superior idea of which candidates to vote for on Election Day because they have a higher level of civic engagement due to their perceived value of their vote (Harrington & Liu, 2002).

People who have college educations also have superior paying jobs, increasing their availability to vote. College education provides the skills that make people more likely to gain the civic skills leading to voting (Valencia, 2005). Attending college increases the person's knowledge of current issues and the candidate's standings to create possible solutions. Increased education and knowledge lead to the voter's assimilation in their communities (Beaver & Chaviano, 2011).

Rolfe (2012) quantified participation in voting as a conditional choice theory that occurs through social networks (Rolfe, 2012). The more educated a person was, and the larger a person's social network would be, therefore increasing a person's voter turnout.

Social ties through higher education are more important than social status within the community (Rolfe, 2012). Rolfe (2012) used this theory to test social structures of how people chose to participate in voting. Difficulty in this method was in documenting and capturing usable data to measure using the conditional choice theory.

Public community organizations and grass root networks can also be tied to ethnicities. The White population is chiefly more educated than the Black and Hispanic populations in the United States (Schneider et al., 2006). Igalens and Roussel (1999) challenged that when variables of socioeconomic status are equal, Blacks and Whites behavior in voting are equal, too. However, Del Pilar and Udasco (2004) stated that the Black population, when engaged politically, was more passionate than the White population in voting. Dutwin et al.'s (2005) study showed that clarifying one's ethnicity when running for political office was vital to increase votes from that ethnicity.

Valencia (2005) stated the ethnic voting theory showed that ethnic identity decreased over time, and the voting behavior increased the longer a person lived in the United States. In 2005, Barreto argued that immigrants in the second, or third generations, who are financially stable and educated, assimilate quickly and vote more. Education and money may seem to make the assimilation a quicker process for the Hispanics that have access to those things.

Hispanics have the lowest voter turnout rates among all the minority groups in part because of the educational gap (Hugo & Taylor, 2012). As Moyo (2009) explains, education provides empowerment and assimilation of all groups when implemented by teachers who know they are working for social justice on behalf of their diverse students. Hispanics could suffer marginalization because their group faces cultural and linguistic barriers in education or even in community activities if not assimilating quickly into local communities (Barreto, 2005).

Religion and Age

Characteristics of religion and age tended to affect people similarly. Researchers Santoro and Segura (2011) showed that individuals who participated in religious activities in the community also tended to vote.

American society, morals, values, and beliefs were developed through the practice of religion and helped institute assimilation for the Hispanics into the community and the polity (Jones & Correa, 2001). Bonilla-Silva and Glover (2006) went further in stating that religious institutions operated both to incubate civic engagements and to recruit congregants to politics through explicit requests for political action. Religious voters are inclined to vote more conservatively than those that did not practice a religion. During the 2012 presidential election, the Obama campaign reached out to African American churches to secure the Black vote to participate by voting for the Democratic Party (Passel, D'Vera, & Lopez, 2012).

Eligible voter means a person who is a U.S. citizen and 18 years old. The largest populations of Hispanic voters were between the age of 18-29 (Hugo & Gonzalez- Barrera, 2012). In 2012, 75 million of the nation's Hispanics were under 18 years of age, and another 83 million were between age 25 and 44 (U.S. Bureau of the Census, 2012)

Among the 18–24 age group, 29% reported being registered to vote, compared to 21 % for the 50–64-year-old group (Hugo & Gonzalez-Barrera, 2012).

The continuous demographic shifts of the American population guided the last two presidential elections from the Republican Party to the Democratic Party. President Obama was able to maintain 67% of the Hispanic vote in 2008 to 71% in 2012 (Hugo & Gonzalez-Barrera, 2012). The 2012 Hugo and Gonzalez-Barrera (2012) polls showed among Hispanics aged

18 to 34 voted for President Obama at a higher percentage of age than conservative Hispanics (Passel, D'Vera, & Lopez, 2012) This election showed that the younger voters tended to be more liberal than their older counterparts. However, of the younger Hispanics born in the Unites States that participated in voting have (25%) higher graduation rates and assimilated better into society (Motel & Patten, 2012/2013).

Characteristics of religion and age played a role when researching who participated in the political process. Religion was similar to education whereas the more a person participated, the more informed they became about the polity. As voter age increased so did participation. The characteristics of religion and age demographics provided insight into the Hispanic voter culture but quantitative research failed to answer why Hispanics lacked participation in the polity.

Summary and Conclusion

This study proposed to examine the lack of participation among Hispanic populations and the characteristics that determined their level of representation in the polity. Quantitative research provided insight but failed to show the underlying reasons that explained why Hispanics remained unengaged in political life. A small-scale ethnographic study could explore the underlying motivations behind this lack of engagement. While limited in scope, this study could provide a fuller and more complete picture of why Hispanics participated at such low rates. The

Hispanic population was one of the fastest growing populations in America. Federal, state, and local governments need to help the Hispanic population assimilate in their communities (Del Pilar & Udasco, 2004). Accepting one's culture and learning how to acclimate to the polity would provide benefits for both Hispanics and the community as a whole (Valencia, 2005).

Hispanic identity has changed over time; redefined multiple times by government through Census categories in ways that demonstrate the marginalization Hispanics. The broader political community is identifying the Hispanics through a system of identification that marginalizes them. Devaluation of their votes occurs because the political community does not want them (Logan, Darrah, & Oh, 2012).

The polity and who gets marginalized in the population defined critical social theory of participation. Empirical literature did not tell us what was the cause of low voter turnout among the Hispanic population. The reason I have undertaken this research was so I could find out the reasons why Hispanics were not participating in the polity, and remaining marginalized by the same polity that provides policies that affect their day-to-day lives.

Generational cultures tended to pass down both negative & positive experiences (Santoro & Segura, 2011). Through qualitative research, the phenomenon of barriers was investigated to find answers to these questions (Battle & Pastrana, 2007). Writing a qualitative ethnographic research proposal would give the reader only a glimpse of the total examination. Researching this topic of analyzing the level of representation of the Hispanic population of the Tom Green County, Texas would give insight, provide possible solutions, and promote social change. Being involved in the polity gives ownership, pride, and self-worth, and it might increase the level of Hispanic representation and identity (Bonilla-Silva, 2004).

TWENTY-THREE

Methodology

Ethnography methodology is qualitative in nature. Ethnography is the appropriate tool to observe people in their day-to-day life. The ethnographic approach aims to immediately create an accurate picture of the group studied and their culture where its specific objective is the new reality that emerges from the interaction of the constituent parts and the pursuit of that structure with its function and meaning (Clarke, 2010).

Ethnographic research includes strategies that are empirical and naturalistic. Nonparticipant and participant observations were conducted to collect data directly related to the detected phenomena. Holistic ethnographic research aimed to construct descriptions of global phenomena in their various contexts and to determine from them the complex connections that affect the behavior and beliefs in relation to such phenomena (Creswell, 2007). Ethnographic qualitative research was a useful method in the identification, analysis, and solution of many problems of public policy (Clarke, 2010). Incorporated into this method of qualitative analysis was the behavior of individuals, their social relations, and interactions with the context in which they develop social relationships (Merten, 2005). These social relationships are important to understanding the importance of the civic engagements and exposure to the polity for the Hispanics. Creswell (2007) described ethnography as a term derived from anthropology, and etymologically it means the study of ethnicity and the livelihood analysis of one race or group of individuals. An ethnographic study was conducted by observing and describing (a) what people do; (b) how they behave; (c) how they interact to describe their beliefs, values, motivations, perspectives; and (d) how these can vary at different times and circumstances. Clarke (2010) observed, "To be engaged in documentation efforts that not only have explanatory power but also connect that power to praxis, we first must contend with the conception that the seeming absence of public action is far from neutral" (p. 10). Observable actions of people in their environment would explain their culture, behaviors, and motivations. Ethnography was the tool used to observe Hispanics in their natural environment.

Seeing how Hispanics interacted with others or me around them has shown how they behaved in their environment. The subjects' responses to my interview questions have helped to explain their motivations, beliefs, and perspectives about low Hispanic voter turnout and civic engagement. I have used ethnographic methodology as the technique for observation, field notes, and data collection. This research was completed in the field with the Hispanic population. Research design for the ethnographic method, according to Moyo (2009), fits well with the relationships between the research questions and data collection.

I have been able to question their participation in the polity, cultural themes, and the Hispanic's political engagement through their eyes. I went into the field and completed interviews. The interview process allowed me to be in the environment with Hispanics who do not participate in civic engagement or have low voter turnout. I looked for the causes of why Hispanics vote at different rates than does other groups. According to Moyo (2009), observing the culture and patterns of individuals I researched was as important as the interview questions. These observations have influenced the conversations during the interviews with the Hispanic population, while looking for answers to why the voter participation is so low in Tom Green County.

Ethnography's purpose is to understand a particular way of life from the point of view of those who belong to it naturally as well as to construct a theory of culture that was distinct to the group (Moyo, 2009). Seeing how Hispanics see themselves has allowed me to discover how their perceptions impact civic engagement in their culture. The goal of using interviews was to capture the vision of the group, their perspective about the world, and the meaning of actions and social situations related to people whom the researcher wants to understand using open ended survey questions (Collis & Hussey, 1997). Merten (2005) stated that in order to understand what the individual is experiencing it is necessary to investigate the impact of the phenomenon. In this context, I was interested not only in what appears to be, but also in what was behind the subject's point of view. Interview questions that allow open-ended responses are an effective means of eliciting responses that can illuminate this point of view. Bryman and Bell (2007) suggested that strategies used in ethnographic inquiry provide phenomenological data representing the worldview of the participants, and these constructs are used to structure research.

Social scientists focus on reality and explain it in different ways, depending on scientific assumptions about what a legitimate perspective was (Creswell, 2007). One way to conceptualize these assumptions was to frame them in four dimensions: the (a) inductive-deductive, (b) subjective-objective, (c) constructive, and (d) generative- enumerative dimensions. I interviewed the subjects while looking for the answers to why the Hispanics do not participate in voting in Tom Green County.

Data Collections and Analysis Plan

During the interview process, I asked the participants questions in a public place and audio recorded the responses using the interview instrument in Appendix B. Consent forms in both English and Spanish were provided and completed prior to the interviews and are included in Appendices B and C. I allotted 1 hour for each interview, but none of the interviews took more than 30 minutes. Data collected from the participant's interviews were analyzed in an issue-focused manner focusing on a lack of voter participation. I conducted each interview in person. Each interview conversation was recorded with a digital recorder and lasted from 5 minutes to 30 minutes. The interviews were conducted on the public sidewalk in front of the grocery store located at 3301

Sherwood Way, San Angelo, TX as previously described in the settings section of Chapter 4. I used the interview questions to stay focused on finding the causes of the lack of voter participation and civic engagement. Implementing an issue-focused analysis gave me the ability to examine the lack of Hispanic voter participation and low voter turnout. I asked questions about their voting participation, barriers to voting, and whether use of public services influences the participation in the polity. Data collected were sorted, coded, and integrated using NVivo. I used the data to analyze the phenomenon of why the Hispanic population does not vote in Tom Green County (Janesick, 2011). Using the issue-focused analysis brought all examined data together so that I could focus on the issue of the study.

Participants and Setting

The ethnographic method was used to study a population of Hispanics not participating in the polity in Tom Green County. Ethnographic qualitative methods helped by evaluating the critical race theory explanation of why lack of voting and community involvement occurs in the Hispanic population Tom Green County (Teddlie & Tashakkori, 2009). Interviews were held in front of the main local grocery store. This site was chosen because it was a diverse heavily populated area, with many people coming and going at all hours of the day. The sample population consisted of Hispanic residents of Tom Green County. I conducted interviews using a standard interview protocol, asking questions of the participants (Janesick, 2011).

The sample population was selected by asking individuals who self- identify as Hispanic individuals to participate in an interview (Creswell, 2009). I asked participants to answer the questions listed in Appendix B. A qualified candidate for an interview was a Hispanic citizen resident of Tom Green County. There was no set number of participants for qualitative research predetermined, but studies that follow this qualitative method tended to reach saturation at approximately 20 people (Creswell, 2009). Therefore, I interviewed 20 people and reached saturation.

One challenge for qualitative research was how to pick the right sample method. Other sampling methods such as random or snowball were available but have ethical constraints to the marginalized Hispanic population. The challenge was that ethical and cultural challenges needed to be considered when dealing with particular ethnic or racial groups, in particular one who is subject to marginalization such as the Hispanic population (Creswell, 2007).

A convenient self-selection sampling method was chosen because I used the individuals available rather than selecting from the entire population of Tom Green County. A Participation Card required participants to self-identify before participating in the interview on the public sidewalk. Random sampling could not be used because the Institutional Review Board required that participants be able to self-identify as Hispanic to participate in the interviews using the Participation Card (Appendix A). Snowballing sampling is when the person initially asked refers a second person who has certain characteristics that may be similar, and this would continue down the sampling line

(Creswell, 2007). When looking at sample choices, a

convenient self-selection nonprobability sample was the least problematic because participants could choose to participate of their own accord. The convenience sampling allowed for the inclusion and exploratory research to discover the details of causes of marginalization and disenfranchisement that exist in the Hispanic population of Tom Green County (Creswell, 2007). I did not have ethical concerns when dealing with this marginalized population because no harm was expected from the study, and the Walden University Institutional Review Board approved my research proposal (IRB approval number 05-04-15-0173408).

Issues of Trustworthiness

I conducted interviews and coded the information collected myself. The interviews were conducted using conventional ethical standards. Participants for the sample were of Spanish speaking origin and some of the participants only spoke Spanish. I am proficient in Spanish and conducted the interview in both English and/or Spanish based on the language preferences of the participant. No level of participant risk was expected in completing the interview. The participants were informed along with instructions that withdrawal was allowed at any time. All participants, prior to signing, read the informed consent form listed in Appendix A, indicating they agreed to be interviewed for this study.

Role of the Researcher

I live in the community in which the phenomenon was occurring. I maintained an etic (outside observer) role in the phenomenon. Conducting this research inside the community provided a subjective analysis of the data I collected (Patton, 2002). Living and working in the Tom Green County, Texas, District 72 has allowed to me gain 28 years of experience with the Hispanic population in the community being studied.

In this study, I submerged myself completing the fieldwork in the Hispanic community by conducting one on one interviews with self-identifying Hispanics and collected data. I used a critical ethnographic method with an advocacy participatory worldview lens when conducting the research (Creswell, 2007, 2009). I created the questions for the interviews and have sole access to all recorded data that were asked of the participants. Questions asked of the interviewee were based in the methodology of qualitative ethnographic study describing and interpreting the cultural or social group's patterns of behaviors, customs, and ways of life (Creswell, 2007). I asked the questions listed in Appendix B to find the answers to these areas of interest in this study.

My role as researcher was to consider all ethical concerns in the study. I used a recording device to record all interviews and to codify all data collected. I have maintained the confidentiality of all participants. I have a background in investigation with training and experience in conducting interviews. I understand how to communicate, using skills from training and experience;

therefore, I have communicated to the sample population the information needed to complete the interviews. The results of the research will hopefully promote social change for the Hispanic population by providing the group access to the polity.

Ethnographic Qualitative Research

Ethnographic qualitative research method has been employed for attaining the authenticated data for the study. This approach gave insight using the research questions concerning the causes of the lack of Hispanic voter participation. Understanding the marginalization of Hispanics in the polity will enable positive social change by increasing awareness to policy makers, activists, and the Hispanic population. Hispanics' civic engagement should acknowledge their needs via understanding lack of voting participation of the population affecting assimilation into the polity. In Chapter 4, I describe how the data collection was implemented and show the results. Appendices A and B are the Informed Consent Form and the Study Survey.

Study Setting

Critical race theory interprets the cultural or social group patterns of behaviors (Crenshaw, 2005). Ethnographic studies require the researcher to conduct field interviews. The location selected for this particular study was the public sidewalk at 3301 Sherwood Way in San Angelo, Texas. The location is in front of the local grocery store where many people of diverse cultures shop for groceries. Many people traverse the sidewalk going to and from the grocery store. I was in a position to select a location that kept me safe from nearby traffic but still allowed me to stand on the sidewalk. The springtime weather was very pleasant until the rain started on the first day of data collection. I stopped when the rain began and then collected data the next day.

Most individuals were very open to reading the participation card (Appendix A) and deciding whether to participate in the interview process. Only a few individuals declined to be interviewed once they had read the participation card. The participation card was provided in English and Spanish (Appendix A). I used a digital recorder and field notes to record the data as I interviewed each participant. I went over the consent form and the interview questions with each participant. Use of the recorder was efficient. A few participants expressed discomfort when I asked them for permission to record the interview. These participants were not aware of a scholarly interview process using a digital recorder. Only two people declined to be interviewed after I asked to audio record the interview. I was able to complete the interviews using a standard interview protocol asking questions of the participants as described in Chapter 3 (Janesick, 2011).

Demographics of the Data Collected

The participant population was the result of a convenience sampling process. The participants were selected from those persons who had come to shop at the grocery store that day. The sample population was asked to self-identify as Hispanic individuals to participate in the interview process, providing the study with a self-selected sample as described in Chapter 3. Participants were interviewed using a standard interview protocol

(Janesick, 2011). As mentioned in Chapter 3, other sample methods were available, but ethical restraints to the marginalized Hispanic population made the convenience self-selecting sampling process the best selection for this study (Creswell, 2007).

Demographics applied to this study included gender, age, occupation, and income.

There were demographic limitations on the potential sample population. Interviewees needed to be over the age of 18 and eligible to vote in Tom Green County, Texas. I interviewed 20 individuals as they walked the sidewalk towards the store or returning from the store after making their purchases.

The participation card in Appendix A allowed individuals to self-select whether or not to participate in the study. Stated on the participation card there was the following: "In order to participate, individuals need to be Hispanic adults, who are 18 years of age and are eligible to vote in Tom Green County and willing to conduct the interview here on this sidewalk." Hispanics eligible to vote are citizens, males or females, over the age of 18, and registered to vote in Tom Green County. Only those who self-identified as meeting this requirement were interviewed.

The table below identifies the demographics of age range and participants. The first demographic variable considered for interview (Appendix D) was gender. I included both male and female participants in this study. Out of 20 participants, eight were female and 12 were male. The second demographic variable considered was the age of the participant. Ages of individuals interviewed consisted of two individuals between 18 to 30 years old, 10 individuals between 30 to 40 years old, three individuals between 40 to 50 years old, and one person between 50 to 65 years old.

Table 5

Age of Participants

Age range	Number of participants
18-30 years old	4
30-40 years old	8
40-50 years old	2
50-65 years old	6

The third demographic question asked the occupation of the participant. The individuals interviewed included an electrician, a retired army veteran, a Texas State Trooper, two stay at home moms, a lawn maintenance company owner, a division director, a contractor, two caregivers, an executive assistant, an advisor, two cooks, a manager, a clinical therapist, a retiree, a hairdresser, a barista, and one unemployed individual. The last demographic question for the interview was regarding the level of income. Of the 20 participants, only two (both in the $30,000 range) would acknowledge their income level.

Hispanics make up over 36% of the total population in Tom Green County; therefore, finding Hispanics entering the location to purchase groceries was not difficult. This location site was chosen because it is a diverse and heavily populated area. The sample population was selected by asking individuals who self-identify as Hispanic individuals to participate in an interview (Creswell, 2007). I was able to question their participation in the polity, cultural themes, and the Hispanic's political engagement through their eyes. The interview process allowed me to be in the environment with Hispanics who do not participate in civic engagement or low voter turnout.

Data Collection

I collected data listed in the interview questions using the approach described in Chapter 3. During each interview, the following questions were asked:

1. Are you registered to vote?
2. Have you voted in the last 6 years?
3. Do you belong to a political party?
4. If so, what party?
5. Could you explain if you do or do not participate in voting?
6. In your experience, are there barriers to participating in voting?
7. If so, what barriers do you see (family, distrust, disinterest)?
8. Have you participated in campaign work?

9. In Tom Green County, only one fourth of those eligible to vote have voted. How would you increase Hispanic voter turnout?

10. Do you use public services such as emergency services, public schools, and or post office?

11. Could you explain how participating in voting could improve those services you use?

I met with the participants on the public sidewalk. While we were out in the open, I was careful to provide the person a private conversation for the interview. I did not allow anyone to stand within hearing range of the person being interviewed. The duration of the interviews of the interviews ranged from 5 minutes to 30 minutes. The overall duration of the interview period was 3 days due to some inclement weather.

I used a digital recorder, the participation criteria card, and survey questions as data collection tools. I used face-to-face interviews with the participants. There were no deviations from the data collection plan.

I collected data concerning the perceptions Hispanics hold about voting in Tom Green County. I used the interview questions to understand their perceptions about voting in the polity and how that affects their community. I also asked about motivations to vote and the characteristics of those who participate in the polity as well as the perceived value of those votes, as discussed previously in Chapter 2 (Harrington & Liu, 2002).

Circumstances encountered in data collection included

failure to interview two people who self-identified but then chose not to participate once I asked to record the interview. These subjects stated that they were nervous and responded that I looked like a cop. The data collection took longer than originally planned due to the unexpected amount of rain in our county during the planned interview period. I complied with the ethics standards related to this study by respecting the participants and adhering to the interview questions that had been approved by the Institutional Review Board.

Data Analysis

In this study, the data centered around the issue of low voter participation from the Hispanic population in Tom Green County. Past researchers have failed to explore, in depth, individual perceptions of why Hispanics participate at low rates in voter turnout. Using an ethnographic study informed by critical race theory (Jacobson, 2001), I sought to interpret the views of the cultural or social group who self-identifies as Hispanic relating to participation in the polity. This approach sought to find barriers that prevent participation in public life (Crenshaw, 1995). This particular study is modeled on the relationships between the research questions and data collection as previously explained by Moyo (2009). The study, designed as described in Chapter 3, observes and respects the culture and patterns of the individuals interviewed.

Data analysis began with transcribing the open-ended

interviews using the NVivo 10 software. The text of the interviews was imported into the package and the resulting information was used to explore the perceptions of the individual participants. As noted in Chapter 3, the interviews were structured to explore individual perceptions of the reasons for and impact of low Hispanic voter turnout. To contextualize the information, the interviews also sought to find out the level of participation in the policy of the participants.

To complete the analysis, I input the audio files and coded the transcripts as described below. I focused the analysis to identify barriers to Hispanics participation in voting in Tom Green County, Texas. The open-ended questions of the interviews yielded a sizeable amount of information related to my topic which was coded to identify the themes raised by the participants. To understand the interviews, I coded the data into themes of similarities of responses from the participants including government distrust, lack of assimilation due to culture, and lack of knowledge and education concerning the voting process. I also included an analysis of discrepant data where individuals offered views that differed from the broader themes. The following explains the process of analysis that occurred.

Input Audio File and Code Transcripts

I have imported audio files to NVivo 10 software and listed and coded the transcripts. I have sorted the primary and secondary data by procedural questions included in the survey. Sorting the data for useful information was my first task. Then, I made verifications. The first verification was to ensure all interviews were complete. At this step, I did not include my viewpoint or opinions. The responses recorded were clear. The responses met the objectives in the research design of why Hispanics do not participate in voting in Tom Green County as discussed in Chapter 2 (Janesick, 2011).

Interview audio files were extracted and saved in a secure file on a thumb drive in a locked filing cabinet for future research as prescribed by the Internal Review Board guidelines. Data collected will be protected to prevent any security breaches as described.

Focusing the analysis

I focused the analysis using each research question and sub-questions to conduct the interviews. The main question was: What barriers keep Hispanics from being fully involved in voter participation?

Sub questions included:

1. Does culture keep Hispanics from fully participating in the civic engagement?
2. What are the barriers to community involvement faced by the Hispanic population in Tom Green County, Texas?
3. What are the reasons behind low rates of registrations and low voter turnout among the voting age Hispanic population in Tom Green County, Texas?

As I worked to analyze the data, I began to look for the interconnection between the answers and a better understanding of the logic behind Hispanic voters not participating in the polity in Tom Green County, Texas. The objective was to improve the depth of understanding of the factors that prevent Hispanics from participating, and to improve that participation in Tom Green County, Texas.

Common answer themes such as discussed previously of government distrust, lack of assimilation due to culture, lack of knowledge and education concerning the voting process, and use of public services began to emerge in the course of data organization. The questions yielded information related to the education of Hispanics and their ideas about the process of voting. Patterns began to emerge that included Hispanics feelings about voting and how voting should be promoted in the community.

Categorizing Information

The data from participant interviews identified several common issues raised by the participants related to voter participation. The responses yielded several common trends in the participants perceptions of voting and civic engagement. The issues raised by the participants fell into several general categories:

1. Barriers within the culture or family.
2. Barriers or marginalization of community involvement.

3. Hispanics use of public services.
4. Reasons behind lack of Hispanic voter participation.

As outlined in Chapters 2 and 3, there is reason to believe that demographic factors could influence the perceptions of the participants. To account for the potential demographic influences on participant responses the interview questions were analyzed using the following demographic criteria as potentially influential factors:

1. Age
2. Gender
3. Income
4. Occupation

TWENTY-NINE

Interpreting Data

Interviewees discussed the need to participate in the polity, however, those interviewed stated lack of education concerning voting and voting procedures stopped them from participating. The examination of perceived impacts of lack of Hispanic voter participation occurred during the research study. The inquiry explored the interconnections within each question. Participants were open in their discussion of the barriers to voting participation and polity participation during the interviews. I found that education concerning the procedures for voting to be a major concern of the participants. Using NVivo 10, following steps listed by NVivo 10:

- Importing my audio files.
- Transcribing the interviews.
- Examining the participant's responses.

- Running a query to determine references.
- Gathering query results and reviewing all material in one place.
- Evaluating the nodes through analysis.

Data interpretation included results to support my theoretical framework listed in Chapter 1. I reviewed past studies included in the literature review for this research. In response to the gap of literature, as discussed in Chapter 2, I developed this research to understand the factors contributing to the lack of Hispanic voter participation in Tom Green County. There is plenty of research data to prove the lack of voting exists by quantitative numbers, however, no one has asked why.

To ensure credibility and dependability of the approach of data consisted of the triangulation of data I reviewed for the literature review. I collected data from multiple resources. The resources included U.S. Bureau of Census, U.S. Federal spending, Texas redistricting, Pew Research Hispanic Trends Project, and Pew Research. National, Texas, and Tom Green County election information were also collected. I made a triangulation of critical information in order to address the lack of Hispanic Voter participation in Tom Green County. I have kept all information gathered and made notes to offer useful recommendations to serve another researcher to conduct a similar study to address dependability (Cresswell, 2007).

Studying the Barriers

Data analysis produced a pattern of the analysis of the interview results themes emerge reflecting how the participants see the key issues this study focused on utilizing the interview process.

The following topics were presented as related to lack of participation included:

- Lack of awareness of the political process on the participant's part.
- Politicians' promises to change the community and does not.
- Not knowing or understanding the voting process.
- Participants suggested voter registration cards needed to include two languages (Spanish and English).

- No initiative in the Hispanic voter community to participate in voting.
- Feeling that votes do not matter.
- Lack of information to Hispanic voters from people seeking office during elections.
- Lack of interest in voting from family that breeds distrust or disinterest.
- Hispanics feel out-numbered, so vote won't count.
- Cultural barriers such as lack of assimilation and familial participation in the polity and civic engagement make Hispanic voters feel embarrassed to participate.
- Of the twenty participants interviewed the following information was obtained.
- 18 consented to be interviewed, 2 declined to be recorded but still wanted to be interviewed.
- There were 12 males and 8 females.
- Individuals from age ranges were four individuals from 18-30 years old, eight individuals from 30 to 40 years old, two individuals from 40-50 years old, and six persons from 50-65 years old.
- The occupations listed by the participants were: Electrician, Retired Army Veteran, Texas State Trooper, two Stay at Home Moms, Lawn Maintenance Co. Owner, Division director, Contractor, two Care Givers, Executive

Assistant, Advisor, two Cooks, Manager, Clinical Therapist, Retiree, Hairdresser, Barista, and an Unemployed Individual.

- Only 2 would tell list their income levels (both in the $30,000 range) the others declined saying it was too personal.
- 12 individuals were registered to vote, 8 were not registered but were eligible.
- 10 of the individuals voted in the last 6 years
- None of the individuals associated with a political party.

Perceived Barriers to Voting

The participants interviewed on the public sidewalk revealed the use of at least some of the public services such as emergency services, post office, and public schools. One potential benefit of increased voter participation is an improved quality of life for the Hispanic population of Tom Green County. As discussed previously in Chapter 2, Hispanics participate in the lowest voter turnout among all the minority groups in part because of the educational gap according to Hugh and Taylor (2012). This study referred to the improved participation rates for Hispanics as the understanding of why to vote increases with education and removal of marginalization.

Participants were asked to name the barriers that prevent participation in the polity, and whether they make use of public services. In the quotes from the transcripts that have been incorporated into this chapter, participant refers to the individual that completed an interview with the researcher. Different issues and perceptions were discussed in relation to this study. The finding here is that the participants answered with mixed messages, stating no there are no barriers, and then explaining what the barriers were for Hispanics. Participants discussed barriers such as lack of education, lack of trust in the government, problems, disenfranchisement and cultural barriers. Also to note, some of the participants stated there were no barriers. With respect to barriers encountered by Hispanics the participants had the following comments. The participant's

answers are in no particular order and included to give insight into the participants answers to the interview questions.

Education as the Barrier

Informant A reported lack of education as a barrier. "No, and if so it's a lack of education. Don't know how to vote."

Informant B reported that lack of education of the voting process affects the process as well as reporting family culture causing disengagement.

"Main barrier is people don't understand the votes does not make a difference, they don't understand the process. So, they think the process is flawed. So, if I vote for white not black or Hispanic instead of whatever they think one vote isn't going to make a difference. It's a learned thing, you learn it growing up, if you parents were voters, then you will vote. If they grow up voting for this person or that person, you will learn to vote. My wife is Caucasian and was raised completely differently than me. My family is completely opposite voting, how we raise children, etc. All that is a learned process from the parents and you usually follow in their footsteps unless you've had a bad experience with one of those process, then you go completely opposite."

Informant C reported lack of education as well as family distrust and disinterest in the community.

"Yes, some, lack of information, to the Hispanic people, no one to explain to them, family, distrust, disinterest —well probably don't vote as well."

Disenfranchisement or Barriers

Informant H reported feeling disenfranchised by the voting polity.

"I feel they don't give us a chance. Hispanics are outnumbered, when we do vote they will never let us have a chance to become something better, don't feel empowered." Informant I reported disenfranchisement of not fitting in with the polity.

"Yes, and thinking there is fear and family embarrassment due to lack of trust in government creating culture barriers. Folks just recently moved here, 2 years ago, with lack of self-confidence and no assimilation, seen as a second-class citizen."

No Barrier

Informant reported no barriers. "No, I don't think there is."

Informant K reported no barriers.

"No, I like the process, it's pretty fair not hindering me." Informants L-S reported no barriers.

"No."

Barriers of Family, Distrust, and Disinterest

Informant B reported the unknowns of politics make eligible voters skeptical.

"Well, I mean what about citizenship, don't their vote do count, loyalties aren't here, so many what ifs in politics."

Informant C reported that trust prevents Hispanics from increasing participation in voting.

"Don't get involved cause no trust, so this doesn't help family from Mexico, don't have that experience in the past, so they don't vote here in America."

Use public services such as emergency services, public schools, and or post office Informant A perception of vote devaluation has discouraged him/her from voting for issues at the local level.

"I have been affected growing up from race. This is what I've noticed. We grow up thinking they don't care about us, even if it's a Hispanic running for office. Why should I vote for local elections, they aren't going to help me out anyway, I already know these people. They won't know where or how to take a

be a party to vote, and add all social media sources, mostly more volunteers."

Informant B reported increasing voter participation would be difficult because of the party lines in Tom Green County.

"That would a difficult thing, the way to increase the Hispanic vote with Tom Green County. Being mostly Republican based unless you go to the border down south, a lot of the Hispanic culture is Democratic. If there was democratic candidate the Hispanic vote would come out, they think and know that the Republican candidate will win, so their nature is Democratic Party so they will not vote. It depends on the individual candidate that wins if the services would change."

Informant C reported that education about the voting process would help Hispanics to be more involved.

"More education toward voting, more advertising, more time to work with Hispanics."

Informant D reported that to increase voting, education would have to interest catching. "I don't know how to increase, issues that affect me, something that grabs my interest."

Informant E reported volunteers are needed to increase education and voting participation.

"Get more people to volunteer take people who translate, and handicap votes, explain the ballot, in different languages."

Informant C reported that informing eligible voters that voting could be done via the mail service increase participation.

"I don't know, maybe being able to vote by mail."

Informant G reported increasing education of voters and the voting system would increase voting participation.

"Well to increase participate you need to get the people to understand what they are voting for, the system now when you listen to politicians they are talking rhetoric not content, and order, the issues are not broken down for you to understand they are disillusioned and it's a long-term process, most people think it doesn't affect me, and most are full of hot air."

Informant H reported increasing education and visiting with recent citizenship graduates would increase voter participation.

"Good question, they have bad numbers, need grassroots level involvement, more education, recent citizenship contacts and those who've been here while. Educating them how to vote, participant in civic things. Many are too busy, can't don't anything about it. I don't think it's a lack of knowing what to do but getting them to think they can be heard.

Do Votes Have Value?

The results of perceptions found among the participants in this study. The study reveals that Hispanics in Tom Green County feel that political representation does not happen because their vote does not have value. Perceptions continue to show marginalization, disenfranchisement, and lack of voter participation.

Gender inequality was also reported in the results. Participants named lack of awareness, broken political promises, language barriers, educational barriers, and cultural barriers as reasons for not taking part in civic engagement or the polity. Participants interviewed represented many different occupational backgrounds that varied in the socioeconomic scale, and although the participants did not wish to share their income, the levels of difference are apparent.

On one side of information participants stated "No, there are no barriers" and yet, the participants went on giving their statement on the barriers that continuously affect the Hispanic participation in the polity. The census of the interviews is that Hispanics don't vote because of "my vote doesn't count so why bother". Bringing forth the information, that although culture is a barrier, Hispanics asked about barriers do not label the existing reasoning as barriers, necessarily. The study found the cooperation of actions is not yet effective between the Hispanic population and voting to have their voice heard (Battle & Pastrana, 2007). Continued lower socioeconomic status of Hispanics makes it difficult for them to compete within the local political organizations. The lack of voter participation seems to stem from marginalization, lack of education, and feeling as if the vote will not matter.

Participants were invited to identify ways to increase voting. Recommendations were suggested that focused attention on education, addressing new citizens, de- marginalization of Hispanics, better civic engagement, advertising directly to Hispanics with Spanish language signs, and offering translators to voters. As discussed in Chapter 2 literature review, these barriers are often over-looked by politicians because of the political parties and candidates tending to focus on long-term party goals (Beaver & Chaviano, 2011). Gerson argued political parties' potential power from the Hispanic voting bloc could be tied to the assimilation level and culture brought into the Hispanic communities (2012).

Interpretation of Findings

In this study, I explored the marginalization and lack of civic engagement of Hispanics in Tom Green County, Texas, District 72. As noted lack of civic engagement is one of the most visible signs of marginalization of the Hispanic population in Tom Green County. Compared to other groups, Hispanics participate in the polity at a much lower rate, resulting in a lack of representation in political life (Chapa & De La Rosa, 2004). Political leaders can afford to ignore or marginalize the Hispanic community so long as it does not hold elected leaders accountable.

I have chosen to explore the perceptions of voting and civic engagement among potential Hispanic voters to fill an important gap in the literature. While quantitative studies have explored general trends in voting and focused on general surveys related to Hispanic voting patterns, these studies have not attempted to understand, in depth, the relationship between perception and political engagement. This study seeks to remedy this through and in-depth exploration of how Hispanic marginalization is reflected in the perception of members of the Hispanic community. The research question at the heart of this study emphasized the perceived barriers impacting Hispanic participation in voting in Tom Green County.

Lack of voter participation in Tom Green County is reflective of the national trend of low Hispanic voter turnout (Texas Legislative Council, 2012). Prior empirical studies of Hispanic voting point to multiple potential explanations for low turnout without agreeing on why Hispanics are not voting. Quantitative studies explore large scale trends and correlations, but do not explain the causal mechanisms of what leaves Hispanics out of the political process. These large-scale studies also tend to miss local factors that may influence Hispanics in the communities in which they live. This study contributes to our understanding of Hispanic voting patterns by engaging in a deeper exploration of the perceptions of members of the Hispanic community in Tom Green County, Texas. This study seeks to provide a deeper explanation as to why we see the larger patterns in the quantitative studies.

The Voting Rights Act of 1965 was meant to remove barriers to voting for all marginalized groups, and Hispanics should have benefited from this change in policy. However, Hispanics continue to be marginalized, and many do not participate in civic engagement. Underrepresentation of the

Hispanic voice denies the group representation proportionate with their population in Tom Green County, Texas.

1. Hispanics' lack of voter participation keeps them from being part of the polity and limits access to the provision of governmental services.

A detailed discussion of the evolution of Hispanic identity and its marginalization in the American polity appears in the literature review in Chapter 2. Several quantitative studies have demonstrated the pervasive pattern of low voter participation by Hispanics in the United States. These studies have offered several, general, explanations for a general lack of civic engagement. Multiple competing explanations for low voter turnout among Hispanics, all supported by empirical research, are discussed in Chapter 2.

Investigation for the literature review showed two main approaches are used to research voter mobilization--rational public choice theory and cultural explanations. However, neither of these approaches measured the perception of barriers among the members of the Hispanic community. My study has helped illustrate experiences for Hispanics that quantitative research could not illuminate because the numerical data available did not explain why Hispanics vote less than others in Tom Green County, only that this lack of civic engagement is occurring.

The theoretical framework discussed in Chapter 1 addressed ethnographic qualitative research as being structured to include small groups of interviewees in naturalistic locations. Chapter 3 described that the interview format used for ethnographic research explored perceptions of participants because it fits well with the relationship between data collection and research questions (Moyo, 2009). The study consisted of two phases of research: (a) investigation of Hispanics' voting patterns and participation in the polity of Tom Green County, and (b) interviews of participants in their naturalistic environment. I used multiple data resources including voting statistics, documents from the United States Census Bureau, literature review, participants' interviews, and observations of the participants to determine disenfranchisement and to protect the disenfranchised (Clarke, 2010). Conducting field interviews allowed me to submerge myself in the environment with Hispanics who do not participate in civic engagement.

Data management went through revision, analysis, categorization, coding, and analysis. Through a triangulation of data, I could ensure credibility and trustworthiness of data (Creswell, 2007). Each research question has been addressed through including relevant quotes from the interviews. Data included the participants saying no there are no barriers to participating in the polity and civic engagement, then explaining that there was indeed an issue. The majority of participants acknowledged the importance of being part of the polity in Tom Green County as well as the importance of voting. From the perspective of the participants, voting is important in order to have the Hispanics' group voice heard; however, culturally, it is not taught amongst the families or community gatherings. Participants perceived this lack of involvement as significant;

however, when speaking about it, they did not believe their individual votes would impact the outcome of the elections.

Discussions about the effects of the lack of voter participation in the Hispanic community has led to other relevant issues that went beyond the primary issues identified in the interview questions. As examined in Chapter 1, Hatch (2002) stated that the researcher who uses qualitative research could create social or political change by providing policy makers with the information collected concerning nonvoting Hispanics. These issues are related to the marginalization of the Hispanic population and the steps needed to create social change within the Hispanic community. The key question was how to create more involvement for Hispanics of voting age population. In this chapter, I discuss the results from Chapter 4. The conclusion of the study and recommendations for social change and future research are included in this chapter.

Interpretation of Findings

The interviews established causalities behind lack of Hispanic voter participation based on that education for voting procedure is not clear to the participants. Participants do not know or understand the voting process, and there is no initiative in the Hispanic voter community to participate in voting or civic engagement.

Disenfranchisement and marginalization were clearly reflected in the responses of the participants. A general perception was that Hispanics were outnumbered by other groups, so their votes would not count. In part this was enhanced by a lack of accurate information about voting and voter registration. Participants were not aware of voter registration being available in the Spanish language or the ability to have the ballot by mail if there was a documented handicap. Participants highlighted evidence of marginalization by the candidates for office. Candidates did not attempt to engage the Hispanic community. Participants noted a lack of information from candidates being directed to the Hispanic population.

Barriers discussed by the participants included familial and cultural distrust of the government and the governmental process of voting. Participants identified politicians who make promises and do not change the community for the better. Cultural barriers contribute to embarrassment within the family and/or community of participation in the Hispanic population. Participants feel embarrassed to vote when they themselves are either not educated on the voting process or being the only one to vote within their group.

Participants identified lack of awareness of the issues concerning public services to be voted on. Participants' knowledge and understanding of politicians elected correlated to the public service and how that affects them. Participants do not believe in or trust the politician in office managing the public service agency to provide services to them or the Hispanic population as promised.

Potential to Improve Hispanic Involvement in Tom Green County

A number of participants acknowledged the ability of Hispanics to mobilize to participate in voting as listed in the results of Chapter 4. A large mobilization would have a significant impact not only on the Hispanic population but also on the outcome of an election in a district where the mobilization takes place. One potential mean for reducing the degree of marginalization of the Hispanic community is to promote engagement in political life through education. Education over civic engagement and teaching the benefits of participating could increase the number of Hispanic voters and assimilation among the community. While this will not end marginalization as a whole, it will improve access to public services and build public sector responsiveness to the needs of the community.

Community activities need to be implemented and structured in a way that produces a significant impact on the lives of the

Hispanic population. One participant stated, "Hispanics are outnumbered, when we do vote they will never let us have a chance to become something better, don't feel empowered." The participants were seeking ways to feel empowered within their community. Educating the voting age population through community activities about voting procedures, locations, and availability of Spanish language ballots would increase voter participation.

The participants responses focus on several important dimensions of Hispanic perception of voting and civic engagement that revolve around information. The general lack of good information about voter registration and voting procedures suggests that better information about the process may reduce the perceived barriers. This suggests that policies designed to improve voter knowledge may be an effective tool for increasing participation. Programs to promote education and recruitment and training of volunteers to educate the Hispanics of voting age could potentially have a significant impact at increasing the perception that voting can change outcomes. In response to the data, I collected a model for volunteer training could include the following:

1. Development of information for organizations focused on education about the voting process.
2. Organization of training for participation in the Hispanic neighborhoods' community activities.
3. Provision of additional training to volunteers in the communities.

4. Implementation of initiatives focused on bringing Hispanics to the polls.
5. Achievement of raising the numbers of Hispanics voting in Tom Green County.
6. Learning from the participation within the community, what Hispanics need at a grass roots level to participate in the polity and vote.

Establishing a framework for measuring participation in voting would contribute to gaining participation from the Hispanic population of voting age and allow for adjustments in a time efficient manner.

Demographic changes are rapidly making Hispanics the largest voting block (Hugo & Taylor, 2012). New perspectives are important to finding why there is a lack of voting participation by the Hispanic population. The results of this study could raise awareness about going beyond the current political education provided to the Hispanic population. Perceptions of the participants of this study suggest that improved education could include improved access the benefits extended to the Hispanic population through civic engagement, participation in the polity, and voting at the polls. Key indicators of improvement of voting by the Hispanic population would be (a) more Hispanic population representation in elected offices, (b) reduced marginalization of the Hispanic population in Tom Green County, and (c) more overall votes by Hispanics at the polls.

Assessment of each of these indicators could lead to future research activities.

Relevance of Hispanics Voting in Tom Green County

The purpose of these interviews was to assess the relevance of Hispanics voting in Tom Green County. In the discussion in Chapter 3, I explained the importance of participating in the polity for the Hispanic population. The Hispanic population fails to participate in voter turnout (Jacobson, 2001). However, voter turnout affects state and federal benefits for business improvement, education, health maintenance, and public safety. As discussed in Chapter 3, the Hispanics make up a significant portion of the population of voters, yet their participation is much lower than their share of the population.

Also at stake are the issues of immigration, affordable healthcare, and education within the Hispanic community. Lack of participation in the election process prevents the Hispanic population from expressing their voice and being fully committed to the political community. The lack of participation also leads to lack of civic engagement and feeling as if their votes will not count. Without education and social change, the much-needed self-sustaining cycle of marginalization would feed a sense that participation was pointless. However, every vote counts, and the education of such should be discussed.

Education in these areas could help with assimilating all citizens to the voting process in Tom Green County, Texas.

Major Challenge of Increasing Hispanic Votes

Effective implementation of education and continuing education is needed to improve Hispanic voter turnout. The findings of this study suggest that although public voter information was available to everyone in Tom Green County, the voting procedure is not being taught in a way that is resulting in Hispanic voters going to the polls.

Changes are needed in public schools and colleges to keep updated with the political process. Avenues of continuing education are needed for individuals who either move to Tom Green, County from other countries or do not attend higher education past high school. The Hispanic population is not participating once they are of voting age. The voting process requires increased bilingual volunteers in the community to participate for the good of the Hispanic population.

Furthermore, the needed education, continued education, the importance of civic duty, community ownership, and how the connection of elections to public services are important in taking steps to de-marginalize Hispanics in Tom Green County. The key finding of this study expresses the lack of participation from the Hispanic population showing the need for education on the elections process. This information will be passed on to State of Texas Representative, Drew Darby for review and hopefully planning to implement changes at a statewide to help locally in improving Hispanic voter turnout.

Limitations of the Study

I identified limitations of the study including not being able to interview all Hispanic Americans in Tom Green County, relying on self-identification, and the process of completing interviews. Interviews were not difficult to conduct in the setting I chose. The weather did become a factor early on but cleared up in time to complete the process. I did encounter a few potential participants who declined either because I look like a police officer or because they did not want the interview recorded. Self-identification was not difficult due to the participation card being used. Also having the participation card read in both English and Spanish made the process more comfortable for Hispanics who could not read English.

The interview process of collecting demographic characteristics produced a limiting factor of individuals not wanting to discuss their incomes. In addition, almost every one of the interviewees stated that lack of education was the heart of the issue with low voter turnout and low civic engagement. I did not encounter any communication gaps or time restraints that were discussed in the limitations.

Recommendations

I recommend building a continuing education strategy within the community to create social change within the Hispanic population about the current political process, issues being voted upon, and to show the Hispanic community desires to participate in the polity. This organization could also provide current education to the Hispanic voting age population to explain the value of one's vote. The outcome of this organization would be Hispanics having their collective community voice heard by voting in elections be not only for education but to recruit the Hispanic population to volunteer giving back to the community.

Future Research

Key recommendations for future research include the following:

1. Assessing the effectiveness of the voting process taught in high school.
2. Encouraging Hispanic community leaders to lead their community to the voting polls.
3. Development of information for organizations to educate Hispanic communities about issues being voted on in the elections.

The assessment of effectiveness of the voting process taught in high school would give insight to the voting process education available through public schools. This assessment would provide useful information about the strengths and weaknesses of the government education classes, including the voting process. The findings would contribute to improve education about voting to all citizens who are near the voting age of 18.

Lastly, research showing the Hispanic community leaders the gaps in their own community could encourage them to share their knowledge with their community.

Community leaders might know that what they do is a reflection of what their community needs but may not realize that more of the community needs to participate in the polity and civic engagement. This education from the Hispanic leaders would be one way to build trust and credibility within the Hispanic community. The trust built through these activities could provide aid for the community through public services once the community understands what is available.

Implications for Positive Social Change

Hispanic Americans are negatively impacted in Texas District 72 and Tom Green County due to lack of political representation. Creating positive social change through increasing voting among Hispanic voter turnout is one way to combat lack of political representation. Civic engagement affects all students and staff in local schools by presenting the students with a positive learning environment (Ingalens & Roussel, 1999). More civic engagement increases ownership of the Hispanic communities and increase political participation and voice. Hispanic leaders can help with informing and motivating the Hispanic people to be involved in the polity through civic engagement and education (Arias et al., 2008).

At the national level, findings of this study may contribute to improving policies that affect the Hispanics and their voting patterns. This study would raise awareness about low Hispanic voter turnout and the implications of lack of civic engagement. The analysis of the Hispanic voter participation would strengthen the capacities of policy makers in setting clear expected improvements for Hispanic communities in Tom Green County and Texas.

At the state level, this study would reinforce information already known, while filling the gap of why Hispanics are not voting. Organizations can improve their models to better fit the educational needs of the Hispanic voting population in Texas. State organizations would be able to use a results-based approach to implement new voter encouragement policies. Organizations would also be able to implement information to build trust and reliability within the communities.

At the community level, the positive social change would be in the impact of changing the Hispanic voting patterns in Tom Green County, Texas. Creating access to information on voting poll accessibility and educating the Hispanic population would provide the county with significant changes in the Hispanic community. Hispanic voters turn out would increasingly show ownership over the entire community.

Theoretical Implications

The ethnographic qualitative theory was used for this research to see the why behind the correlations of lack of participation in voting by the Hispanics (Creswell, 2007). Qualitative theory asserts the researcher to place the findings in the context in order to understand and create social change among the

Hispanic population. Chapter 2 Literature review outlined the problems contributing to the prohibition of Hispanic participation in voting in Tom Green County. The ethnography focused on culture, relationships, and societal views of the lack of Hispanic voter participation in Tom Green County (LeCompte & Priessle, 1994). The interviews were completed in a natural location, which encouraged the respondents to respond truthfully. Logan, Darrah, and Oh (2012) identified low voter turnout to have characteristics of low socioeconomic positions, however, the results of this study showed lack of participation related to many types of jobs or careers levels. The data from the interviews confirmed the classification of Hispanics, and the disenfranchisement is occurring through their identification and their position in the polity. As discussed in Chapter 2, the interviews did reflect what Hispanics in the county feel (Mertens, 2005). The majority of the informants stated that barriers where not apparent then identified barriers being one of the issues among the polity. Informants believe the structure of the elections and politics are corrupt and their vote would not matter or help change the issues.

Summary

Marginalization of Hispanics is one of the biggest challenges of Tom Green County, Texas, District 72. The marginalization of Hispanics is also one of the largest challenges facing America as the Hispanic population continues to grow. The state population of Texas in 2010 was 25,145,561 in which 37.6 % or 9,460,921 are Hispanic (Texas Legislative Council, 2010). The U.S. Bureau of the Census (2012) identified 18.28 million Hispanics as the largest minority group in Texas, making up 33.6% of the voting age population. In Texas District 72, the total voter age population of the Hispanic population makes up 24.1% or 22,011 Spanish surname registered voters. Tom Green County has a population of 104, 010 people. 84,290 of those residents are in the voting age population and 31% or 26,516 are Hispanic Americans (Texas Legislative Council, 2010). In the 2012 elections, the Hispanics voter age population only 2,430 or 16%

turned out to vote (Texas Legislative Council, 2010 Census, Red 236, p. 6). Analyzing the Hispanic population's involvement in the community to understand voter mobilization characteristics determining the level of participation by the group in the political process is necessary (Dutwin et al., 2005).

In America's federal system, political participation takes place at the federal, state, and local level. Lack of participation in all three of these levels can lead to a lack of attention from political leaders and the marginalization of non-participating groups. Groups compete for scarce resources in the political space. Americans want government to provide social benefits such as welfare, food stamps, and health-care-- all of which can benefit the Hispanic population (Arias et al., 2008). Hispanics continue to be marginalized from participating in voting concerning these critical social benefits, leading to a situation in which Hispanics consistently get fewer resources than the groups with which they compete. To have a voice, Hispanics must increase rates of voter participation in order to provide representation commensurate the size of their population. Hispanics need to articulate their desires and demands to their politicians via the ballot box.

This study sought to deepen our understanding of why Hispanics do not participate in political life in a local community--Tom Green County at the rates we would expect given their significant presence in the population. Explanations based on the concepts of extrinsic and intrinsic rewards have been considered in past research on barriers Hispanics encounter when voting (Dutwin et al., 2005 & Pink, 2009). I selected the questions to observe this phenomenon through the cultural lens of critical race theory (Patton, 2002). Critical race theory allowed me to study the role of race and inequality in the Hispanics of Tom Green County's society and their participation in civic engagement levels (Johnson & Onwuegbuzie, 2004).

To explore the perceptions that underpin the lack of participation required participant interviews to understand how these perceptions contribute to the marginalization of the group (Clarke, 2010). The interviews in this study allowed a detailed exploration of the role of perception for a small number of participants. These responses contextualize and extend the findings from larger-scale studies into macro- trends in the national and state Hispanic populations.

Quantitative studies such as those by Santoro and Segura (2011) and others listed in Chapter 2, used measures of classic assimilation collected through a national survey to analyze empirical data on the likelihood of Hispanics being marginalized. However, these empirical studies fail to identify the barriers or offer solutions. I have chosen qualitative research method to explore the "why" Hispanics lack participation in the polity. Researchers have identified psychological theories as determining factors of why people do not act; however, the research had not been done to find the barriers (Pink, 2009). This study is qualitative and asks the participants the barriers affecting their voting participation instead of focusing on the large-scale quantitative surveys.

It is shown that critical race theory lens has helped to find the racial differences that have been normalized to the point of invisibility (Price, 2010). The barriers identified by the participants are so ingrained in their society, the participants would state that there were no barriers, then go on to list the barriers by name – education, disenfranchisement, culture barriers, family distrust and disinterest. Showing the Hispanic population of Tom Green County, the marginalization could lead to their participation in the voting process as described.

The methodology of the ethnographic approach created an accurate picture of the group studied. The behavior, social relations with family, and interactions in the community were considered when writing the interview questions asked. I conducted the data collection in a public space as to provide a group of participants. Individuals were asked to self-identify using a participation card.

Qualified interviewees were Hispanic citizens of Tom Green County of voting age. I used issue-focused analysis to bring all the examined data together to focus on issue and gain the results listed. The study identified influences on the Hispanic population of Tom Green County as those of family, education, and cultural barriers.

Current news, social media biases, and miss informed individuals create the need for factual continuing education Hispanics through civic organizations is of utmost importance. Participants suggested the following ideas, when asked how to increase voting in Tom Green County, increased translators, voting ballots in Spanish Language, advertising focused on the Hispanic community, informing the voters of issues at hand, and most important education. The community of Tom Green

County could create social change through educating the Hispanic population with alliances with non-profits, along with government agencies local, state, and federal.

The research study was conducted to seek answers to the underlying reasons that explain lower voter turnout in Tom Green County. Using field interviews, the participants shared their perceptions of barriers and ways to increase voting in Tom Green County. I looked at the interconnection presented by the participants' answers concerning barriers within culture and family, lack of community involvement, and lack of education as reasons why Hispanics do not participate actively in the polity. The participants stated use of at least some of the public services and benefits from living in the community of Tom Green County. The results identified an educational gap as one reason of low voter turnout, confirming the discussion of Hugh and Taylor's findings in 2012. When investigating the gap in literature, and interviewing participants on the lack of voting by the Hispanic community the forgoing conclusion is education. Education of the Hispanic population of Tom Green County could give the pride of ownership and authority to civic groups and individuals in the community who share common beliefs, morals, values, and thoughts through participation in the polity; providing the right to create social change in the environment in which they live in.

SEVEN

Updated Presidential Election Data

Since publication of the dissertation in August 2015 America has had the 2016, 2020 presidential elections and early voting starts in less than a month with the 2024 Election. There's been increases in Hispanic voter turnout in each of these elections. The County of Tom Green and the city of San Angelo are two locations researched above since they service a wider area known as the Concho Valley. Tom Green County and San Angelo are in Federal Congressional District 11. District 11 has a citizen voter age population 517,419 which Hispanics are 28.4%. comes to a potential 146,947 Hispanic voters that could vote.

In general elections of 2012 Hispanic voter turnout was 20.3% of 334,142 of those which is 67,830. In general election of 2016 Hispanic voter turnout was 22.3% of 377,692 of those which is 84,225. In general election of 2020 Hispanic voter turnout was 23.7% of 459,342 of those which is 108,864 in Federal Congressional District 11 in Texas. In the dissertation we looked at Texas House of Representatives District 72. Each time we look at data of Hispanic voter turnout in area of Tom Green County including San Angelo, Texas has a lower voter turnout of Hispanics than the state and national averages.

In August 2024 with the continuing technology advancements in cell phones, apps, social media platforms such as TikTok is increasing information to those marginalized. Social & News media are lying to the people in America and around the world. Fake social and news media post also effect those who serve our country and Mark Zukerberg of Facebook has stated in a written certified statement August of 2024. Elon Musk has made it clear after purchasing Twitter and releasing documents FBI and federal government were banning things pro-Trump.

PART II
Social and News Media's Affect on Law Enforcement

Social and News Media's Affects On Law Enforcement

This is an investigation of how social and news media's false reporting affects law enforcement. Law enforcement is experiencing increases in resisting arrest, physical assaults, and murders by subjects targeting the police. These increases of criminal behaviors have law enforcement de-policing within the communities, and the catalysts are social and news media's false reports that police officers are racist. A content analysis was used to investigate the literature on social and news media's effect on law enforcement and criminal behavior. The data focused on articles in peer-reviewed journals, published research articles, and social and news media reports. The results are societies perceptions are influenced by false reports (fake news) by social and news media outlets. Individuals who react to the fake news either using threats, assaulting, or murdering of police officers. In return, law enforcement's workplace environment becomes more dangerous causing de-policing, increasing in violence, and criminal behavior.

Introduction

Violent crime rates in the United States are escalating as law enforcement is de-policing (Wolfe & Nix, 2016). Responsibility has been placed among several high profiled new reports of cases involving law enforcement officer shootings. However, this study investigates false narratives of these crisis events by the media leading to numerous protests as well as increases in violence that are negatively affecting law enforcement. Police officer's shootings of African Americans since 2014 including Michael Brown August 2014, Laquan McDonald October 2014, Tamir Rice November 2014, Walter Scott April 2015, and the arrest as well as deaths of Eric Garner July 2014, Freddy Gray April 2015, and Sandra Bland July 2015 have challenged the legitimacy of law enforcement (Wolfe & Nix, 2016). When crisis situations such as the Michael Brown case in Ferguson, Missouri, a falsified report of "hands up don't shoot" are amplified by social and news media inciting citizens to overreact with violence toward their communities by stimulating comments of "burn this motherfucker down" and targeting of police officers throughout America.

Individuals and groups use social and news media to stream movies, media platforms, and the news on current events (Thongjeen & Wormeli, 2017). Social and news media outlets such as CNN, Fox News, Facebook, and Twitter have platforms where news and people post information on current events. Citizens are increasing the use and adoption of the social and news media to participate in events as never before (Huang, Starbird, Orand, Stanek, & Pedersen, 2015). "Little is known, however, about the dynamics of the life cycle of a social media rumor" (Zubiaga, Liakata, Procter, Wong Sak, & Tolmie, 2016). As media outlets occupy people with reports of events there is evidence of increasing criminal behavior, lack of personal responsibilities, and tolerance towards others.

These false reports are triggering more individuals and groups to commit criminal behavior targeting law enforcement. Targeting of law enforcement consists of increased resisting arrest, assaults using bottles and rocks, to murder by assassination. Of the last 10 years 1,512 law enforcement officers have died, an average of one death every 63 hours or 151 deaths per year in the line of duty (National Law Enforcement Officer Memorial Fund, 2017). These reports have been correlated to on-line outcries and revenge attacks on police officers (MacDonald, 2016). Data collected from the FBI reports 86 Officers were killed, and 50, 212 officers were assaulted in the line of duty in 2015 (FBI, 2016). Targeting of police officers is just one part of the phenomenon. Social and news media false reports affect officers as well as criminal behavior. "Violent crimes are increasing as criminals reassert themselves due to the Ferguson effect and de-policing of law enforcement (MacDonald, 2016).

MacDonald (2016) states, "de-policing and crime in the wake of Ferguson: Racialized changes in the quantity and quality of policing among Missouri police departments." Instead of racial profiling citizens, police officers are the ones being targeted. Before the Ferguson effect homicides were at a twenty-two-year low. Homicides spiked nationally 17 percent across 50 of the largest cities in 2015. Furthermore, larger cities had a 12 percent increase in homicides and cities of less than ten thousand in populations had an increase of 7 percent. Murders of police officers also increased to 135 in 2016 due to reports of officer's shootings of Black males. (Shjarback, Pyrooz, Wolfe, & Decker, 2017)

Americans already distrust government as the media provides 24 hours a day coverage focusing on crisis events where citizens become emotional lashing out through protest or worse, more violence. The media continue speculation on the numbers of causalities, their injuries, and types of weapons used during these events. The false news further damages trust, beliefs, emotions, and behaviors of individuals and groups among our communities (Green & Clark, 2013). For example, the individuals who protested for days destroying their community over the Michael Brown case in Ferguson, Missouri found the reports by the social and news media were false (MacDonald, 2016).

Recently, a considerable number of protests turned violent injuring participants, vandalized city blocks, looting of businesses, and burned down buildings within the communities (James, 2015). Social and news media outlets no longer report unbiased news. Media's false narratives of events not only increased distrust but also are increasing the criminal behavior

(MacDonald, 2016). Media reporting of news stories are based on ratings; therefore, reports of events are quickly published without fact checking, nor providing the reference in order to have a greater emotional impact on the potential audience (Stone & Socia, 2017). Examples range from a police officer involved shootings of a black male, hate crimes involving homosexuality, or reports of a political leader accused of sexual assault (Brown, 2016). Social and news media report speculation on events and citizens believe every word to be true.

"Much of what we know and think we know comes not from personal experience but from the stories we hear" (Dirikx & Bulck, 2014). One of the main challenges is individuals act out against those falsely accused from the media's untrue reports. There is evidence that supports media's false reporting increases individual's negative attitudes as well as actions toward law enforcement across America. Police officers are among those being falsely targeted, attacked, and killed by individuals as well as groups acting out based on media reports. July 2016 an individual ambushed the Dallas Police Department killing 5 officers and injuring 9. The motive of the assassinations was correlated to crisis events reported by the media of police officer-involved shootings of black males. Police officer's jobs are to protect and serve to provide for safer communities, and yet they are the ones needing protection. (MacDonald, 2016)

For this study, action research was used to investigate a social phenomenon, consults with stakeholders' input on the situation, and implement positive change. This study addresses two questions: (1) how does social and news media false reporting of events affect law enforcement? (2) How does social and news media false reporting of events affect criminal behaviors? The purpose for this study is to conduct action research to gather a greater understanding of the phenomenon of how social and news media's fake news affect law enforcement in order to offer solutions reducing false reporting by the media, decrease criminal behavior, and decrease the dangers law enforcement are facing every day.

THIRTY-NINE

Methods

LITERATURE INVESTIGATION PROCESS

Literature for this research was obtained by searching the Angelo State University Library, Google Scholar, Goolge.com, and PEW Research Center databases. Review for literature was completed searching articles published since 2013. The year 2013 is correlated to the current trend of increased violence toward police officers as social and news media outlets report false narratives. The focused of this research was uncovering articles on social and news media's reporting of fake news and its affect on law enforcement. The author will not focus on social media posts written by the general public. That topic will be another article published in the future. This study investigates outlets for social and news media reporting of events in order to analyze, how people reacted after receiving false narratives toward the law enforcement as well as criminal behavior.

Relevant keywords for this study include social influences,

news influences, media influences, affects on law enforcement, fake news, false news, false reporting, criminal behavior and social media, affects on criminal behavior, police officer shootings, social media protesting, and news media influences on websites such as (Twitter, Facebook, Snapchat, YouTube, Instagram). The preliminary search for articles totaled 1,084. There are 211 relevant articles investigating the use of social and news media in society.

Much uncertainty is still apparent on social and news media's affect on law enforcement as well as criminal behavior. Gaps were apparent within the majority of the literature over social and news media's false narratives and how they affect law enforcement. The literature consisted of 211 articles on research topics ranging from; individuals using the Internet determining guilt or innocence behind the keyboard, On-line gossiping of famous actors and actresses, and social media outlets such as Twitter being used during major disasters. Media's actions must be investigated to understand the scope of reporting fake news and the damage that occurs to law enforcement.

Social and news media outlets surpass fact-checking the legitimacy of reports to be first (Andrews, Fichet, Ding, Spiro, & Starbird, 2016). Reporting first on major news stories produces ratings. Technology advancements in mobile devices virtually allow anyone to report the news through social media platforms. Podcast, YouTubers, Facebook personalities or other social media platforms bring society information non-stop. The virtual media environment continues changing the way Americans learn about the news. Social and news media outlets have complicated reporting the news as they try to stay in control of what people hear, see, or listen to around the world. In order to make a determination of this the social phenomenon, this study used a critical action research methodology to investigate, gain greater understanding, and to provide solutions in order to decrease fake news, violence and to save lives.

FORTY

Literature Analysis

Previous criminological studies used both qualitative and quantitative methods to provide greater knowledge on social and news media. Narrowing down of articles relevant provided literature over the following themes: perceptions of the community, how media frames an event and comparing Twitter to mass media watched on television when disasters strike. The quantitative methods provide numerical data to analyze causation of crime as well as make predictions of behaviors using social media, and the qualitative research provided insight on methods and data strategies to use on social media, but the literature review did not justify the gap on how fake news affects law enforcement. "Regardless of the size of the dataset or the number of variables contained within it, quantitative data can only represent abstractions from complex interactions, and as Bottomley and Pease (1986) remind us, 'we should not allow statistics to make us forget the people behind the numbers" (Wincup, 2017).

Framing News Reports

Fragmenting factual evidence on events such as a police officer shooting of a black male by the media increases criminal behavior and violence (Lee & Thien, 2015). Framing signifies the approach social and news media use to report events. When the media frames the facts falsely on an event the law enforcement officers are targeted with threats of violence, assault, and murdered. The media mediates their reports controlling the narrative of events. The public consumes the news reports as truthful information. Researchers Tool & Fondacaro (2017) state, "the media depicts young offenders as subhuman" in order for the community to understand juvenile criminal behaviors. The framing of juveniles in this event negatively labels them. Tool & Fondacaro (2017) state, "Journalist are beginning to engage in conversations about their contribution to American crime culture". The media knowingly and intentionally reports fake news allowing the dehumanizing of juveniles, misrepresenting facts, and increasing criminal behavior as well as targeting of police officers. But we still need to understand why.

Another research study was on 12-year-old boy Tamir Rice who was shot and killed by police and framing by the media was crucial on how society reacted (Stone & Socia, 2017). Where does the media place blame when police shoot a 12-year-old boy playing with a toy gun? Social and news media framing of reports blamed the police officers that deployed the use of force without knowing the facts. Stone & Socia (2017) states, scholars have identified stereotypical frames used for news to promote general hostility toward African Americans". Stone & Socia go on saying the stereotypical response occurs to fulfill the audience expectations and reinforce negative stereotypes (Stone & Socia, 2017). The social and news media framing of facts in order to satisfy the stereotypical expectations of the audience could be a manipulation of the truth as well as a violation of the law.

Twitter Post Disasters

Research on social and news media has provided platforms for individuals to communicate during disasters. Subjects could post information on weather conditions, devastation, number of injuries, and other medical conditions. Researchers Huang, Starbird, Orand, Stanek, & Pedersen (2015) states, "Widespread adoption of social media has enabled members of the public to participate in disaster events as never before." Investigating individuals' use of social and news media during disasters provides information in real time for those in authority to respond. The reliability to analyze the data was a key variable with social media users. Gathering data during a live disaster in order to respond with emergency services relies on the validity of the person sending the information.

Numerous research studies have investigated the use of

Twitter during disasters, elections, sporting events, and cases involving police officer shootings of black males. The research on the use of Twitter identifies the quickness people cluster, use of hashtags #'s, and themes versus specific current events. Twitter leads media platforms for individuals engaging on-line when events occur (Smith, Rainie, Himelboim, Shneiderman, 2014). Barthel, Mitchell, & Holcomb (2016) research shows 71% of Americans have witnessed fake news reports online such as Twitter, and 100% of the individuals stated they shared the fake news. (Barthel, Mitchell, & Holcomb, 2016)

Individuals and groups believe what the media reports causing further distrust as well as criminal behavior toward law enforcement. After reviewing the literature there is still a gap of knowledge on the affects of fake news on police officers. False reports by the media and its affects on law enforcement warranted a qualitative study. Action research method was used to understand how social and news media's fake news affects law enforcement, criminal behavior, and to create potential solutions saving lives while decreasing crime.

Results

Participation in social and news media in America consist of over 320 million users (Perrin, 2015). The criminal justice system can no longer ignore social and news media outlets as 56 % of the U.S. population carries a video-enabled smartphone, and 65% of those are adults using the mobile devices to get their news (Perrin, 2015). Misinformation is a regular occurrence based on the fast-paced environment of news reporting process. Although information on social media was repeatedly unverified, the social and news media outlets are trying to report stories across the world for ratings. Nonwhites and the less educated increasingly say they get news on social media by 74% (Bialik & Matsa, 2017). Fake news from social and news media causes confusion and anger on the basic facts on events. Although 32% of people think social and news media is made up, 84% of them are confident in their abilities to recognize fabricated news (Bialik & Matsa, 2017).

"Americans are much more likely to see posts related to race or race relations than they are to personally post or share race-related content" (Anderson & Hitlin, 2016). Blacks account for 13.3% or 43,320,000 of the 325, 719,178 in population in the United State population as of July 2017. Researching social media comparing whites, and Blacks; 28% of Blacks social media users state, most or some of what they post is about race or race relations and 8% of whites say the same. Interestingly, there are over 500 million tweets each day, and 0.04% mention race, but yet the news media reports as if 99% of America is reacted to a crisis on race (Anderson & Hitlin, 2016). Comparing Twitter posting to the television news outlets generates the headlines deciding what events are reported, and how that event is framed for consumption. In the Michael Brown case in Ferguson, Missouri; a friend of Brown's gave an interview stating Brown's hands were up and the officer shot Brown anyway. Reaction to Twitter was a spike in tweets to over three point five million tweets, but yet the television news outlet only reported the event an average of 98 minutes in the same 24-hour time period (Hitlin, 2014). On-line social and news media platforms are taking the lead compared to the news on the TV.

Law enforcement agencies in America do not have the resources to police the Internet at a local, state, or federal levels. As social and news media outlets increase from demand and technology so does the dangers. Researchers Stone & Socia

(2017) state, "members of the Online News Association found that members were concerned that the growth in the online news was threatening to the fundamental values of journalism, citing loosening journalist standards, declining accuracy, and increased emphasis on speed". Internet sites such as Facebook, Twitter, Snapchat, Instagram, or YouTube provide worldwide platforms for individuals to a network as they consume information that is open source. When social and news media sites report events such as a police officer involved shooting, they lack checks and balances and at times report fake news (MacDonald, 2016). Social and news media current trend of growing online also provides implications of the ability to report more events, but less follow up stories. The lack of follow up stories in the news decreases for facts to be verified or corrections to be published (Stone & Socia, 2017).

Outrage from the community many times begins with social media. The fake news in the Michael Brown case with "Hands Up Don't Shoot" was a total falsified report. Yet social and news media quickly ran with that portion of the story focusing on a young black male unarmed was shot to death by a racist police officer even when Brown had his hands in the air. But that was not factual, and after a federal investigation, several witnesses stated that Brown didn't listen to the officer and continue to act violently. The falsified report of Brown's hands were up and saying don't shoot lead to massive protest as well as riots broke out in Ferguson, over 25 buildings burned, over 150 shots fired by rioters, patrol cars were burned completely, 13 individuals injured, 80 individuals arrested, and one fatality. That's not the total story. Michael Brown protests turned violent across the country from Los Angeles to New York all from one falsified report. (Hitlin & Vogt, 2017)

Targeting of Cops

Fake news reports on events resembling police officer shooting of black male subjects by social and news media are escalating tensions as well as reactions by the public. Media's false narratives have affected targeting of police officers by increasing the number of attacks, and the number of ambushes killing officers. When social and news media report the fake news the majority of individuals respond on Twitter with negative comments or threats of violence. As the falsified reports spread people begin to take action first through social media campaigns with hashtags, then participate in "death in's" laying face down in the street and protesting blocking police stations. As tensions continued to rise so did the use of the social and news media reporting of speculation. Citizens believe the fake news is sowing confusion as events occur (Barthel, Mitchell, & Holcomb, 2016).

August 9th, 2014, police officer Darren Wilson shot Michael Brown in Ferguson Missouri that triggered tensions and protests within the community. Social and news media reported false facts and witnesses' accounts. The abuse of reporting fake news by the media turned a protest into violent riots and looting. The riots turned into terroristic acts when rioters began burning of buildings within the community to attain political goals through instilling fear. The acts of terrorism were said to justify the shooting of a black male by police. Social and news media were used to escalate the tensions as well as the reaction of the public.

As social and news media continue reporting false narratives criminal behaviors will continue to increase. Individuals among American society retaliate against others where the media places the blame. FBI released a statement warning people making threating comments using social and news media "to watch those social media post or face the consequences" (Malagon, 2017). The FBI gathers data on police officers that are killed in the line of duty. The data over targeting police officers steadily increased from 5 officers being ambushed in 2013 to 21 officers being ambushed in 2016. The FBI data goes on giving unprovoked killing of officers in 2013 was 0, and in 2015 there were 7 officers unprovoked but were murdered. Comparing data between the shootings, committed by either police or by subjects there are more deaths by police officers committing the act. However, to understand the data we must look at the totality of the facts. Each year the law enforcement community has over 50,000 on duty officers physical assaulted. October 2016, 57,180 police officers were victims of the line-of-duty assaults (FBI, 2017).

Since 2014 FBI has documented 40 ambush cases of police officers murdered (Hjelmgaard, 2016). In 2016; 21 ambush-style attacks occurred and 20 of them ensued in November. Conducting an examination of social and news media around the time when a police officer was killed, there had been racially charged events that lead to the targeting of the officers. Cases involving police officers being ambushed:

- Douglas County Sheriff's 1 officer killed & 4 injured Dec 2017.
- Dallas Police 5 officers killed & 9 injured July 2017.
- Des Moines Police 2 officers killed November 2016.
- New York Police 2 officers killed December 2014.
- Las Vegas Police 1 officer shot November 2015.
- Ferguson Police Department 2 officers shot March 2015

As social and news media continues reporting false narratives violence toward law enforcement continues to climb (Laughlin, 2017). As individuals use their devices non-stop, they become cyber-intolerant targeting others wrongfully accused. Fake news reports are being used for political and business agendas as well as justification for individuals who commit criminal behaviors. There are more questions than answers when researching fake news reports in the media.

FORTY-TWO

Discussion & Conclusion

Law enforcement officers are serving across America under great pressure to maintain peace while protecting the law. Peace Officer's lives are in countless danger as individuals' make threats or attacks increases. Social and news media outlets use platforms such as Facebook, Twitter, Instagram, YouTube, and Snapchat to inform the people of current news as it occurs. That same media falsely reports information speculating on what is true while racing to be first in reporting current events as they unfold. The media fails in fact check information continuing to release fake news for individuals to consume, and the media does not care how people react toward those wrongfully accused. Once the falsified information is released people react by posting negative comments on socials and news media platforms, make threats, protest, and attack causing injuries to murder. The media rarely remedies fake news when facts are finally apparent.

The research literature continues to give evidence on why mass media reports false narratives. The evidence points to the social and news media outlet's agendas are creating rating, therefore; the media caters to the demographics (Stone & Socia, 2017). Either way, when we analyze the fake news from social and news media, we must hold them accountable for the damage that occurs. False reported information is a crime, and fake news causes individuals and groups to react in negative ways increasing criminal behaviors.

As the nature and volume of crime changes the criminal justice system must advance their abilities in cyber intelligence. Forensic criminology of today's society with advances in technology the criminal justice system lacks the resources and funding. The criminal justice system needs resources including people, training, and equipment to fight back the abilities of social and news media outlets to manipulate the facts of the events.

Over 5 million tweets were posted of comments as well as information on the shooting of Michael Brown by police officer Darren Wilson. The Ferguson Police Department did not have the ability to investigate the Twitter data on the case. Individuals connected by tweeting each other on Twitter about where and when to protest, riot, or loot, and yet law enforcement didn't have any idea this was occurring. At this time there is no way to monitor all activities on social and news media observing reactions posted by individuals who post. The criminal justice system needs as up to date as possible the resources to be better equipped mentally and physically. Repetition develops efficiency and police officers are a part of authority as well as first responders that need this training the most.

Force on force will not remedy the issues between law enforcement and the people. Building communication communities could begin the healing of the division among our society. Communication communities are defined as people of the community take ownership within their community working with local government, as well as law enforcement to become better stewards of society. The government, law enforcement, and other organizations would bond together with all people in the community creating a partnership. This partnership would spread out personal and professional responsibilities starting with communicating with each other of needs, wants, and future outcomes.

One component in creating the communication communities would be to educate citizens on falsified reports and how responding negatively damages themselves by potently breaking the law or causing riots destroying their own communities. Expectations, as well as the rule of law, need to be clear on how each partner will act. Citizens and media outlets should both demand accountability to the reporting of falsified information. Individuals or media who falsify a report or target police officers will be dealt with swiftly and harshly. The Criminal Justice System must be held accountable as well, as they are the authority serving and protecting citizens in American.

There is a culture within the social and news media

organizations, government agencies, political parties, groups, and individuals that are underneath dishonesty of justice as they continue to report the fake news. In recent past, America's last presidents used fake news to bend the blame to win reelection in 2012. Most recently the 2016 Presidential Elections had enormous amounts of fake news trying to change voting outcomes. When news reports are misconstrued people across the world accept that information as fact. At the same time, individuals, as well as groups that are usually marginalized, are no longer. Social and news media platforms have opened the door for social change to occur by those marginalized. One marginalized person could use a hashtag #, comment, post, video, or a picture that could change the world.

EIGHT

American Elections 2024

Thursday June 27th, 2024 was the Presidential debate on CNN, UGH.

As a political science professor, we need to document the facts about our generations being deranged stressing the heck out as fake social and news media platforms are being controlled by the American government. Every time there is a crisis here in America or abroad, I do my best to collect at that time data by recording the news, videos and relevant post. Download as much as you can to research later and watch who and how the narratives changes. Yes, facts change, and truths get updated. Watch how disinformation is being used. Who's hiding the truth and has caused. Hmm, caused? See, I feel like a victim, because I bought in to the American Dream, the ideal that if I participated in the polity helping others paying forward then they GOVERNMENT and LAW would be fair and honest.

Instead, they have been using the American people sending us to wars losing hundreds of thousands of lives, and crippling millions more with mental and physical damages. I have been a mouthpiece spreading history and standing up for America in cases only to find out the President of the United States lied to me.

American People, we're "living on edge." There's dishonesty in the world today, and everyone knows it's wrong. American leaders are using different perceptions, and perspectives than you and I. Therefore, we need to LEARN some "definitions."

Art II Section II of the United States Constitution gives the authority to the president of the United States to nominate the heads of over 4000 agencies that help run our government for the people. The Senate shall give advice and consent to the president's nominees by two thirds of the senators present concur. Each agency has their own standard operating procedures and policies that they go by.

Therefore, the 438 agencies each have definitions within their standard operating procedures of what is an imminent threat? After 107th United States Congress passed The Patriot Act under President George W Bush a month after 9/11 extended federal governments authority to preeminent strikes a person or group who pose an imminent threat to the United State of America or it's interest anywhere in the world. The president's branch continues using his own definitions for terms that should come from the constitution United States or other policy written by the Congress but that might not be the case.

Technology advancements generate reality out of

imagination with breakthroughs in communication worldwide like digital currency, video chats, even in gaming. Adobe voice software can be used to create deepfakes with eight spoken syllables. Social and News Media platforms are using all the above to control the narratives, but why?

The Founding Fathers wrote the U.S. Constitution and amended it with a Bill of Rights expressing the Freedom of Speech and the Freedom of Press. The Founding Fathers never imagined digital footprints, geotagging, encrypted iPhones, and Ai. Each President of The United States including the Biden Administration tries to control the narratives in order to accomplish their ideologies and agendas.

The Biden administration is using their own set of definitions to run the world. An example would be President Biden saying the United States is not at war with Russia. Biden has asked and signed into law 200 billion dollars to Ukraine in military aid to attack, I mean to defend Ukraine's sovereignty against Russia. Yet, the boundaries of the playing field and the definitions used to describe the theater of war mutate day-to-day depending on the social and news media used to report the happenings.

How do we live in transparency? Transparency does not mean truth. It's not always factual. There're "media" attacking Tucker Carlson saying he's a racist from discussing the N word, vulgarness, crimes, gender, color, and economic status; whatever variable we want to stick in there others want to have the use of free speech banned.

Discussing opposing views over topics as if the person is

committing the crime is not American. Freedom of speech is being banned by United States Congress concerning who killed Jesus? Banning free speech— how is that justified, how is that free?

When training as a firefighter, law enforcement training, or basic education you'll learn; it's against the law to yell fire in a movie theater, but government doesn't ban the word. Where does it stop?

In 2010 under President Obama, Congress passed Obamacare gutting healthcare in America raising costs. Obama came out saying, "Your insurance isn't going to cost you a dime." People on one side said, you're lying, you're full of it, the other side says, no, he's telling the truth. What's the truth? Was President Obama telling the truth? Technically, he didn't lie. Until you can find one person who pays a dime for insurance, he's told the truth.

Therefore, we have a ghost government, a shape shifting American government trickling all the way down into city governments as politicians begin to have mob mentality. How are we the American people going to deal with this? As of July 30th, 2024, there's plenty of drama in 2024's election cycle, but at what cost?

Throughout my academic tenure teaching political science, security studies and criminal justice I repeatedly saw correlations in history. Mentors and historians claim history repeats itself and we're seeing this play out as of July 13th, 2024. In 2018, a batch of JFK files were released allowing information on Watergate, JFK assassination, Martin Luther King assassination, Robert Kennedy assassination, and all the dramatic events in the 60s and 70s that ultimately changed the course of America.

There seems to be more connections between the deep state and abuse of presidential powers found every day in my research. During World War II our President FDR had authority to bend the rules leading America out of the Great Depression, and lead into world war from an attack on one American ships by Israel. That's what helped the creation of term limits and twenty fifth amendment.

Like the gossip from Biden wanting to alter SCOTUS; FDR wanted to pack the Supreme Court of the United States after not getting his way with laws being passed. I believe it's a bluff tactic at this time to steer away from fact Biden shouldn't be running the country if he's unfit for reelection.

Remember, we have to ask the right questions to get the answers we are wanting to know. American government agencies such as the FBI, CIA, EPA, and other Executive Branch agencies (hire contractors do all America's dirty work) to cause conflicts, regime changes, and wars since at least since World War II.

During the Revolutionary War, the Founding Fathers used newspapers and pamphlets as their media to persuade the colonial people to go to war against Great Britain. The Civil War used the Morse code to communicate, America's mail system over time has been used to correspond across the nation throughout magnitudes of crisis since 1775. The Founding Fathers manipulated the public using freedom of the press, FDR did it, Eisenhower, Nixon, JFK, LBJ, Obama, the list goes on. We are learning more and more as I dive deeper into different areas of my expertise. Nixon was involved with manipulating narratives using the mafia, and Cuban nationals to carry out certain agendas by way of freedom of the press.

How can one be ready to die for America when we find out that the America that we've always been told does great things is flipping leaders of other countries to get their way— actually killing these people taking them out like Vietnam, and Korea, and Iran. America even tried to assassinate Castro. When you start adding up these pieces begin to ask questions such as was Nixon involved in JFK's assassination? More details are coming out while diving way past what I learned at the universities. Even at the PhD level. Can you believe the mafia, CIA, and a president got together and try to take out Castro by assassination him in 1960 when Nixon was vice president for Eisenhower.

So, if in 1960 Nixon and others are willing to assassinate Castro—the leader of a Cuba, what's to say in November of 1963 the same people or group didn't do it to our own leader? You might say, oh that's not right, America couldn't do that well. Research America's involvement with the Shah in Iran following coup in 1953. How many leaders of other countries or companies have American CIA, or CIA operatives, from our government pays someone from another country, or even in our own country to take them out? *Note* I wrote this paragraph before July 13th, 2024.

The agenda to publish this book was to update the dissertation and research articles that were published in 2015 and 2019 as the major drama from President Trump running for office. I also wanted to update the research to observe if the potential solutions and ideas that have been implemented since publications. The America's political environment in 2024 is setting the bar for the most disenfranchised voters in history of the country with the Democratic party skipping over the fourteen million voters in the primaries and have the delegates online choose a front runner that has never won a single primary as president of the United States of America in 2024. In this format I wanted to share studies giving insight on what has occurred over the last ten years compared to where America was in 2000. Remember this isn't America's first drama election, just most current one.

America, *We The People* must have public virtue earning our citizenship preserving our union through participating in the polity to keep it free as possible.

Voter Identifications are NOT harmful to ANY ELECTION unless it is rigged.

NINE

Public Virtue

Americans are not all educated equally. People must take personal responsibility. Individuals who take ownership in their community through civic engagement by attending meetings, participating in watch programs, and serving boards have sense of belonging as well as pride which encompasses The American Dream.

Elected officials and government employees must be held accountability as do political parties, corporations, non-profits, social, and news media platforms by enforcement or by creating new laws not to infringe on American's civil liberties or guaranteed rights by The United States Constitution. Public officials in or running for office could be held personally responsible for lying by using technology to monitor their body metrics. Tech giants already monitor and collect keystrokes, things we say near cellphones, computers, and other digital devices. Therefore, body metrics technology to fight against corruption in who spends trillions of dollars to spread democracy while killing millions of people for those running for office might be a step in the right direction.

There must be a balance of advancing our society or committing crimes against the America people. We The People are given authority by the U.S. Constitution to have a republic type of government if We the People can keep it as Dr. Franklin stated coming out of the constitutional convention when asked, but the problem is government has been allowed to get too big. We The People must take back their authority by participating in the polity. Communication is the correlating factor. In order to fix communication, we need to create what I call communication communities. We The People must be able to communicate to our local, state, and federal governments directly helping accountability.

Communities across our nation download apps to their devices communicating back in forth, playing games, and to see what's happening in the neighborhood. Why not utilize technology with advocating the expectations engaging the community beyond talking by creating a welcome to our community post with hands on activities and community engagement they can do together enriching the culture of our society. Citizens of the community can educate other citizens on current topics, jobs, goods, and services, and local agencies can introduce expectations of local ordinances and laws as well as introduce those who will be protecting and serving their communities.

Incorporating everyone in belonging in our communication communities by having public virtue first helping others. Social gatherings using social media, monitoring streets, community clean ups, local businesses supporting other local businesses, as well as a pass it on attitude would generate generational wealth for generations to come. We the people have a duty to contribute in order form a more perfect union.

TEN

Who Wins 2024?

Today is October 2nd at 3:23am in the morning, I couldn't sleep. My Editor & Publisher Michelle Morrow of Publishology asked me to sleep on it. Take one more night to make sure I've made all changes before uploading to publish. Bedtime was at 12:26am. I laid there going over my day. The debate with Senator Vance, and Governor Walz was on YOUTUBE. Again, my thoughts go to should I include the debate to be as current as possible. That is who I am.

The time has come to give what I think will be the outcome of America's twenty-twenty four Presidential Election and who will win. Early voting has begun in Virginia, Minnesota, South Dakota, Pennsylvania, and Texas early voting begins October 21st 2024. My research perception and theoretical lens looked at what do the marginalized individuals voices need in the community I lived and worked. I found in our community the Hispanic population is not voting. I wanted to know why. Interviews from participates wanted Trump back in office.

Hispanic Americans are wanting to separate themselves from those coming across the broken border. Hispanic Americans want a booming economy from a president. Do the polls on social and news media reflect this? No. As of October 2nd 2024 270 to win shows Harris wins Electoral College 292 to Trump's 246. Gallup's Party Affiliation Poll show Democrats down 6% in September 2024. This is the first time more Republicans are out registering Democrats since 1992.

Rasmussen Reports on X, September 30th 2024, shows Trump at 49% of likely voters compared to 46% for Harris. Then we go to the Nate Silver Report and algorithm of current polling, events to predict a winner. After running thousands of times using all factors plugged into The Nate Silver Method determines a winner by percentages of times one candidate wins over the other. Nate Silver Report shows Harris has a 53% chance of winning the election.

Swing states local polling show Trump, Harris are tied. Social media, podcast, YouTubers, have turned toward Trump after visiting in long format with interviews lasting hours, compared to Harris's avoidance live media. The Fake News chooses Harris.

Together including our street knowledge, my experiences show at this time Harris will get 273 Electoral College votes to Trump's 265. Trump might get the popular vote. I hope am wrong and Trump wins for the boost to economy. I do not have faith in the people of America to vote Trump back in office after 2020's Pandemic.

References

Americanization of race relations in the United States. In M. Krysan and A. Lewis (Eds.), The changing terrain of race and ethnicity (pp. 149-186). New York, NY: Russell Sage Foundation.

Anderson, M., & Hitlin, P. (2016). Social media conversations about race: How social media users see, share and discuss race and the rise of hashtags like #BlackLivesMatter.

Antunes, G., & Gaitz, C. M. (1975). Ethnicity and Participation: A Study of Mexican- Americans, Blacks, and Whites. American Journal of Sociology, 80(5), 1192- 1211. doi:10.1086/225950

Arias, E., Schauman, W. S., Eschbach, K., Sorlie, P. D., & Backlund, E. (2008). The validity of race and Hispanic origin reporting on death certificates in the United States. Vital and health statistics. Series 2, Data evaluation and methods research, (148), 1-23.

Barthel, M., & Shearer, E. (2015). How do Americans use Twitter for News? Pew Research Center, 1-7.

Barthel, M., Mitchell, A., & Holcomb, J. (2016). Many Americans believe fake news is sowing confusion. Pew Research Center, 15.

Barreto, M. A. (2005). Latino immigrants at the polls: Foreign-born voter turnout in the 2002 election. Political Research Quarterly, 58(1), 79-86.

Battle, J., & Pastrana, A. (2007). The relative importance of race and socioeconomic status among Hispanic and White students. Hispanic Journal of Behavioral Sciences, 29(1), 35-49.

Beaver, K. M., & Chaviano, N. (2011). The association between genetic risk and contact with the criminal justice system in a sample of Hispanics. Journal of Contemporary Criminal Justice, 27(1), 81-94. doi:10.1177/1043986210396205

Bernard, R. (2006). Social research methods: Quantitative and qualitative approaches. Thousand Oaks, CA: Sage.

Bialik, K. & Matsa, K. (2017). Key Trends in Social and Digital News Media. Pew Research Center

Bonilla, Y., & Rosa, J. (2015). # Ferguson: Digital protest, hashtag ethnography, and the racial politics of social media in the United States. American Ethnologist, 42(1), 4-17.

Bonilla-Silva, E. (2004). From bi-racial to tri-racial: Towards a new system of racial stratification in the USA. Ethnic and Racial Studies, 27, 931-950.

Bonilla-Silva, E., & Glover, G. (2006). "We are all Americans": The Latin

Bowler, S., Nicholson, S. P., & Segura, G. M. 2006. Earthquakes and aftershocks: Race, direct democracy, and partisan change. American Journal of Political Science, 50(1), 146-159.

Brown, G. R. (2016). The blue line on thin ice: Police use of force modifications in the era of camera phones and YouTube. The British Journal of Criminology, 56(2), 293-312.

Bryman, A., & Bell, E. (2007). Business research methods (2nd ed.). New York, NY: Oxford University Press.

Cacciatore, M. A., Scheufele, D. A., & Iyengar, S. (2016). The end of framing as we know it... and the future of media effects. Mass Communication and Society, 19(1), 7-23.

Callahan, V. J. (2012). Media consumption, perceptions of crime risk and fear of crime: Examining race/ethnic differences. Sociological Perspectives, 55(1), 93-115.

Carney, N. (2016). All lives matter, but so does race: Black Lives Matter and the evolving role of social media. Humanity & Society, 40(2), 1-20. Doi: 10.1177/0160597616643868

Castillo, C., El-Haddad, M., Pfeffer, J., & Stempeck, M. (2014, February). Characterizing the life cycle of online news stories using social media reactions. In Proceedings of the 17th ACM conference on Computer supported cooperative work & social computing (pp. 211-223). ACM.

Chagnon, N., & Chesney–Lind, M. (2015). "Someone's been in the house:" A tale of burglary and trial by media. Crime, Media, Culture, 11(1), 41-60.

Clarke, K. (2010). Toward a critically engaged ethnographic practice. Current Anthropology, 51(S2), S301-S312. Retrieved from http://dx.doi.org/10.1086/653673

Collis, J., & Hussey, R. (1997). Business research (2nd ed.). New York, NY: Palgrave Macmillan.

Crenshaw, K. (1995). Introduction. Critical race theory: the key writings that formed the movement (pp. xiii-xiv). New York, NY: New Press.

Creswell, J. (2007). Qualitative inquiry and research design: Choosing among five Approaches (2nd ed.). Thousand Oaks, CA: Sage.

Deardorff, K. E., & Blumerman, L. M. (2001). Evaluating components of international migration: Estimates of the foreign-born population by migrant status in 2000 (Population Division Working Paper Series No. 58). Washington, DC: U.S. Census Bureau.

Del Pilar, J. A., & Udasco, J. O. (2004). Marginality theory: The lack of construct validity. Hispanic Journal of Behavioral Sciences, 26(1), 3-11.

Derickson, K. D. (2016). The racial state and resistance in Ferguson and beyond.

Dirikx, A., & Van den Bulck, J. (2013). Media use and the process-based model for police cooperation: An integrative approach towards explaining adolescents' intentions to cooperate with the police. British Journal of Criminology, 54(2), 344-365.

Donovan, K. M., & Klahm IV, C. F. (2015). The Role of entertainment media in Perceptions of Police Use of force. Criminal Justice and Behavior, 42(12), 1261-1281.

Downs, A. (1957). An economic theory of democracy. New York, NY: Harper and Row.

Dutwin, D., Brodie, M., Herrmann, M., & Levin, R. (2005). Latinos and political party affiliation. Hispanic Journal of Behavioral Sciences, 27(2), 135-147.

Erlach, D. (2000). Hispanics and higher education: Multicultural myopia. Journal of Education for Business, 75(5), 283-295.

FBI (2016). FBI Releases 2015 Statistics on Law Enforcement Officers Killed and Assaulted. https://www.fbi.gov/news/pressrel/press-releases/fbi-releases-2015-statist...

Farmer, A. K., Sun, I. Y., & Starks, B. C. (2015). Willingness to record police-public encounters: The impact of race and social and legal consciousness. Race and Justice, 5(4), 356-377.

Gerson, M. (2012, September 24). Republicans are missing an opening with Hispanic voters. The Washington Post. Retrieved from http://72.washingtonpost.com/

Groves, R., & Vitrano, F. (2011). The decennial census and the ACS: Looking back and looking head. Presentation at the Population Reference Bureau. Retrieved from 72.prb.org

Harrington, L., & Liu, J. 72. (2002). Self-enhancement and attitudes toward high achievers: A bicultural view of the independent and interdependent self. Journal of Cross-Cultural Psychology, 33, 37-55.

Hatch, J. A. (2002). Doing qualitative research in educational settings. Albany, NY: State University of New York Press.

Hess, K., & Waller, L. (2014). The digital pillory: media shaming of 'ordinary' people for minor crimes. Continuum, 28(1), 101-111.

Hitlin, P., & Vogt, N. (2014). Cable, Twitter picked up Ferguson story at a similar clip. Pew Research Center.

Hitlin, P., & Holcomb, J. (2015). From Twitter to Instagram, a different# Ferguson conversation. Pew Research Center, 6.

Holcomb, J. (2014). Where was Ferguson in my Facebook Feed?

Huang, Y. L., Starbird, K., Orand, M., Stanek, S. A., & Pedersen, H. T. (2015, February). Connected through crisis: Emotional proximity and the spread of misinformation online. In Proceedings of the 18th ACM Conference on Computer Supported Cooperative Work & Social Computing (pp. 969-980). ACM.

Hugo, M., & Taylor, P. (2012). Latino voters in the 2012 election. Washington, DC: Pew Hispanic Center.

Igalens, J., & Roussel, P. (1999) A study of the relationships between compensation package, work motivation and job satisfaction. Journal of Organizational Behavior, 20(7), 1003-1025.

Jacobson, L. (2002). Recalibrating voter turnout gauges. National Journal, 34(3), 196- 198.

James, N. (2015). Is violent crime in the United States increasing. Congressional Research Service, 7, R44259.

Janesick, V. J. (2011). "Stretching" exercises for qualitative researchers. Thousand Oaks, CA: Sage.

Jones-Correa, M. (2001). Institutional and contextual factors in immigrant naturalization and voting. Citizenship Studies, 5(1), 41-56.

Jurkowitz, M., & Vogt, N. (2013). On Twitter: Anger greets the Zimmerman verdict. Pew Research Center.

Kerbel, M. R. (2005). American government: Your voice, your future. Cincinnati, OH: Atomic Dog.

Kort-Butler, L. A., & Habecker, P. (2017). Framing and Cultivating the Story of Crime: The Effects of Media Use, Victimization, and Social Networks on Attitudes About Crime. Criminal Justice Review, 0734016817710696.

Laughlin, B. (2017). Police Swamped with False Reports. Daily Inter Lake.

Lee, H., Lee, Y., Park, S. A., Willis, E., & Cameron, G. T. (2013). What are Americans seeing? Examining the message frames of local television health news stories. Health communication, 28(8), 846-852.

Lee, S. T., & Thien, N. P. (2015). Media, race and crime: Racial perceptions and criminal culpability in a multiracial national context. International communication gazette, 77(1), 24-50.

Leighley, J., & Vedlitz, A. (1999). Race, ethnicity, and political participation: Competing models and contrasting explanations. Journal of Politics, 61(4), 1092-1105.

Leiva, A., & Bright, D. A. (2015). "The usual suspects": media representation of ethnicity in organized crime. Trends in Organized Crime, 18(4), 311-325.

Liang, Z. (1994). Social contact, social capital, and the naturalization process: Evidence from 6 immigrant groups. Social Science Research, 23(4), 407-437.

Liao, F. (1994). Interpreting probability models: Logit, probit, and other generalized linear models. Thousand Oaks, CA: Sage.

Lien, P.-T. (1998). Does the gender gap in attitudes and behavior vary across racial groups? Political Research Quarterly, 51(4), 869-895.

Logan, J. R., Darrah, J., & Oh, S. (2012). The impact of race and ethnicity, immigration and political context on participation in American electoral politics. Social Forces 90(3), 993-1022.'

Lopez, M. (2008). The Hispanic vote in the 2008 election. Pew Hispanic Center. Retrieved from http://72.pewhispanic.org

Malagon, E. (2017). The FBI has seen an increase in online threats across the country. Chicago Tribune.

Matsa, K. E. (2016). Facebook, Twitter play different roles in connecting mobile readers to news.

Mac Donald, H. (2017). The war on cops: How the new attack on law and order makes everyone less safe. Encounter Books.

Maslow, A., & Frager, R. (1987). Motivation and personality (3rd ed.). New York, NY: Harper and Row.

McNutt, P. A. (2002). The economics of public choice (2nd ed.). Cheltenham, UK: Edward Elgar.

Mertens, D. M. (2005). Strategies for qualitative research. Research and evaluation in education and psychology: integrating diversity with quantitative, qualitative, and mixed methods (2nd ed., pp. 239-241). Thousand Oaks, CA.: Sage Publications.

Mitchell, A., Gottfried, J., Shearer, E., & Lu, K. (2017). How Americans Encounter, Recall and Act Upon Digital News. Pew Research Institute.

Motel, S., & Patten, E. (2012a). A record 24 million Latinos are eligible to vote, but turnout rate has lagged that of Whites, Blacks. Pew Hispanic Center. Retrieved from http://72.pewhispanic.org

Motel, S., & Patten, E. (2012/2013, December 9). On immigration policy, deportation relief seen as more important than pathway to citizenship: A survey of Hispanics and Asian Americans. (Appendix A). Pew Hispanic Center. Retrieved from http://www.pewhispanic.org/2013/12/19/on-immigration-policy-deportation-relief-seen-as-more-important-than-citizenship/

Murray, S. (2009, June 22). Numbers on welfare see sharp increase. The Wall Street Journal, Business News and Financial News. Retrieved from http://online.wsj.com

Nedelmann, B. (1987). Individuals and parties' changes in processes of political mobilization. European Sociology Review, 3(3), 181-202.

O'Connor, K. W., & Schmidt, G. B. (2015). "Facebook Fired" Legal Standards for Social Media–Based Terminations of K-12 Public School Teachers. Sage Open, 5(1), 2158244015575636.

O'Toole, M. J., & Fondacaro, M. R. (2017). When school-shooting media fuels a retributive public: An examination of psychological mediators. Youth Violence and Juvenile Justice, 15(2), 154-171.

Pantoja, A. D., Ramirez, R., & Segura, G. M. (2001). Citizens by choice, voters by necessity: Patterns in political mobilization by naturalized Latinos. Political Research Quarterly, 54(4): 729-750.

Passel, J., D'Vera, C., & Lopez, M. (2011). Census 2010: 50 million Latinos:

Hispanics account for more than half of Nation's growth in past decade. Washington, DC: Pew Research Hispanic Trends Project.

Patton, M. Q. (2002). Qualitative research and evaluation methods (3rd ed.). Thousand Oaks, CA: Sage.

Perrin, A. (2015). Social Media Usage: 2005-2015: 65% of Adults Now Use Social Networking Sites--a Nearly Tenfold Jump in the Past Decade. Pew Research Trust.

Pew Research Hispanic Trends Project. (2004, July 22). The 2004 National survey of Latinos: Politics and civic participation. Washington, DC: Author.

Pew Hispanic Center. (2010). Mapping the Latino electorate. Retrieved from http://pewhispanic.org

Pink, D. (2009). Drive: The surprising truth about what motivates us. New York, NY: Riverhead Hardcover.

Pitman, B., Ralph, A. M., Camacho, J., & Monk-Turner, E. (2017). Social Media Users' Interpretations of the Sandra Bland Arrest Video. Race and Justice, 2153368717705420.

Plano Clark, V. L., & Creswell, J. (2008). The mixed methods reader. Thousand Oaks, CA: Sage.

Press, P. J. (2008, May 28). Texas Hispanics lack clout at polls. San Angelo Standard- Times [San Angelo].

Price, P. L. (2010). At the crossroads: critical race theory and critical geographies of race.

Procter, R., Crump, J., Karstedt, S., Voss, A., & Cantijoch, M. (2013). Reading the riots: What were the police doing on Twitter? Policing and society, 23(4), 413-436.

Progress In Human Geography, 34(2), 147-174.

Pyrooz, D. C., Decker, S. H., Wolfe, S. E., & Shjarback, J. A. (2016). Was there a Ferguson Effect on crime rates in large US cities? Journal of criminal justice, 46, 1-8.

Rainie, L. (2014). The six types of Twitter conversations. Pew Research Center, 20.

Rodolfo, O., & Cortina, J. (2007). Are Latinos Republicans but just don't know it? The Latino Vote in the 2000 and 2004 presidential elections. American Politics Research, 35(2), 202-223.

Rolfe, M. (2011, December 15). Voter turnout: Political economy of institutions and decisions (Kindle ed.; Kindle Locations 4016-4017). New York, NY: Cambridge University Press.

Rosenfeld R., Gaston S, Spivak H, & Irazola S (2017). Assessing and Responding to the Recent Homicide Rise in the United States. National Institute of Justice

Rowe, M. (2013). Just like a TV show: Public criminology and the media coverage of 'hunt for Britain's most wanted man'. Crime, Media, Culture, 9(1), 23-38.

Sanchez, G. R. (2006). The role of group cohesion in political participation among Latinos in the United States. American Politics Research, 59(3), 435-446.

Santoro, W. A., & Segura, G. M. (2011). Generational status and Mexican American political participation: The benefits and limitations of assimilation. Political Research Quarterly,64 (1), 172-184.

Schier, S. E. (2003). You call this an election? America's peculiar democracy.

Schneider, B., Martinez, S., & Owens, A. (2006). Barriers to educational opportunities for Hispanics in the United States. Hispanics and the future of America, 179-227.

Segura, G. M., & Rodrigues, A. (2006). Comparative ethnic politics in the United States: Beyond black and white. Annual Review of Political Science, 9, 375-395.

Simanski, J., & Rytina, N. (2006). Naturalizations in the United States, 2005.

Schulenberg, J. L., & Chenier, A. (2014). International protest events and the hierarchy of credibility: Media frames defining the police and protestors as social problems. Canadian Journal of Criminology and Criminal Justice, 56(3), 261-294.

Shearer, E. & Gottfried, J. (2107). News Used Across

Stevens, D., & Bishin, B. (2011). Getting out the vote: Minority mobilization in a presidential election. Political Behavior, 33(1), 113-138.

Social Media Platforms 2017. Pew Research Center.

Stone, R., & Socia, K. M. (2017). Boy With Toy or Black Male with Gun: An Analysis of Online News Articles Covering the Shooting of Tamir Rice. Race and Justice, 2153368716689594.

Thomas, A. J., & Blackmon, S. K. M. (2015). The influence of the Trayvon Martin shooting on racial socialization practices of African American parents. Journal of Black Psychology, 41(1), 75-89.

Thongjeen, P., & Wormeli, P. K. The Impact of Social Media on the Police Organization and the Challenges the Police will face in this Digital Era.

Teixeira, R. A. (1987). Why Americans don't vote: Turnout decline in the United States: 1960-1984. Westport, CT: Greenwood Press.

Texas Redistricting. (2012). Retrieved from http://www.tlc.state.tx.us/redist/districts/house.html

Tom Green County. (2011). County A in the western part of Texas: Elections results. San Angelo, TX: Author. Retrieved from http://co.tom-green.tx.us/ips/cms/othercountyoffices/Elections/Election_Results/index.html http://co.tom-green.tx.us/default.aspx?

Tom-Green County/Elections. Results Valencia, R. A. (2005). What if you were first and no one cared: The appointment of Alberto Gonzales and coalition building between Latinos and communities of color. Washington and Lee Journal of Civil Rights and Social Justice, 12, 21.

Van Hook, J., Brown, S. K., & Bean, F. D. (2007). For love or money? Welfare reform and immigrant naturalization. Social Forces, 8(2), 643-666.

Verba, S., Schlozman, K. L., Brady, & Nie, N. (1993). Race, ethnicity and political resources: Participation in the United-States. British Journal of Political Science, 23, 453-497.

U.S. Bureau of the Census. (2011). Voting and registration in the election of November 2010: Tables (p. 20). Retrieved from http://census.gov

U.S. Bureau of the Census. (2012). Census Bureau Homepage. Retrieved from www.census.gov

US Federal Government Spending as % of GDP: (n.d.). US Federal Government Spending as % of GDP (Quarterly, Percent of GDP). Retrieved June 16, 2014, from http://ycharts.com/indicators/govt_spend_gdp

Weitzer, R., & Kubrin, C. E. (2004). Breaking news: How local TV news and real-world conditions affect fear of crime. Justice Quarterly, 21(3), 497-520.

Wondemaghen, M. (2014). Media construction of a school shooting as a social problem. Journalism, 15(6), 696-712.

Wong, J. S., Lien, P.T., & Conway, M.M. (2005). Group-based resources and political participation among Asian Americans. American Politics Research, 33(4), 545- 576.

Yardley, E., Lynes, A. G. T., Wilson, D., & Kelly, E. (2016). What's the deal with 'websleuthing'? News media representations of amateur detectives in networked spaces. Crime, Media, Culture, 1741659016674045.

Zercoe, C. (2017). 10 Keys to Managing the Narrative of a Critical Incident Capture on Body Camera

Taylor, P., Gonzalez-Barrera, A., Passel, J., & Lopez, M. (2012, November). An awakened giant: The Hispanic electorate is likely to double by 2030. Washington, DC: Pew Hispanic Center.

Tannahill, N. (2012). Texas government (12th ed.). Upper Saddle River, NJ: Pearson Education.

Teddlie, C., & Tashakkori, A. (2009). Foundations of mixed methods research: Integrating quantitative and qualitative approaches in the social and behavioral sciences. Los Angeles, CA: Sage.

Pew Research Hispanic Trends Project. (2004, July 22). The 2004 National survey of Latinos: Politics and civic participation. Washington, DC: Author.

Stray, J., Iyer, R., & Puig Larrauri, H. (2023). The algorithmic Management of Polarization and Violence on social media.

Teixeira, R. A. (1987). Why Americans don't vote: Turnout decline in the United States: 1960-1984. Westport, CT: Greenwood Press.

Texas Redistricting. (2012). Retrieved from http://www.tlc.state.tx.us/redist/districts/house.html

Tom Green County. (2011). County A in the western part of Texas: Elections results. San Angelo, TX: Author. Retrieved from http://co.tom-green.tx.us/ips/cms/othercountyoffices/Elections/Election_Results/index.html.http://co.tomgreen.tx.us/default.aspx? Tom-Green_County/Elections.Results

Valencia, R. A. (2005). What if you were first and no one cared: The appointment of Alberto Gonzales and coalition building between Latinos and communities of color. Washington and Lee Journal of Civil Rights and Social Justice, 12, 21.

Van Hook, J., Brown, S. K., & Bean, F. D. (2007). For love or money? Welfare reform and immigrant naturalization. Social Forces, 8(2), 643-666.

Verba, S., Schlozman, K. L., Brady, & Nie, N. (1993). Race, ethnicity and political resources: Participation in the United-States. British Journal of Political Science, 23, 453-497.

U.S. Bureau of the Census. (2011). Voting and registration in the election of November 2010: Tables (p. 20). Retrieved from http://census.gov

U.S. Bureau of the Census. (2012). Census Bureau Homepage. Retrieved from www.census.gov

US Federal Government Spending as % of GDP: (n.d.). US Federal Government Spending as % of GDP (Quarterly, Percent of GDP). Retrieved June 16, 2014, from http://ycharts.com/indicators/govt_spend_gdp

Wong, J. S., Lien, P.T., & Conway, M.M. (2005). Group-based resources and political participation among Asian Americans. American Politics Research, 33(4), 545- 576.

Zur, H., & Hatuka, T. (2023). Local–digital activism: Place, social media, body, and violence in changing urban politics. Social media+ Society, 9(2), 20563051231166443.

About the Author

Shawn Morrow, M.ED., Ph.D., a Publishologist of Political Science, Security Studies, and Criminal Justice investigates and reports on the use of fake social and news media effects on society and encouraging citizens to participate in our polity.

Dr. Morrow encourages everyone to stand up & speak out with their voices while continuing to participate in our communities.

facebook.com/ProfessorShawnMorrow

Also by Shawn Morrow, M.ED., Ph.D.

Articles

The Effects of THC on Depression, New Mexico's Influence Magazine. (March 2023)

The Growing Cannabis Culture in New Mexico, New Mexico's Influence Magazine. (Nov 2022)

Social & News Media's Effects on Law Enforcement. Global Journal of Forensic Science & Medicine Ireland Publisher" (May 2019)

Stinnett, Jean & Morrow, Shawn S. The Keeper. Sundance Festival's MAST Studio (March 2019)

Marginalization of the Hispanic Population & Law Enforcement" International Organization of Social Sciences and Behavioral Research "IOSSBR" (March 2019)

Social & News Media's Effects on Law Enforcement. International Organization of Social Sciences and Behavioral Research "IOSSBR" (March 2018)

Causes of Low Voter Turnout of the Hispanic Population in Southwest Texas (August 2015)

How MMA Changed My Life, Train Hard Fight Easy Magazine (August 2013)

Books

I am Not Going to Be Your Alibi (January 2023)

In Honor of a Veteran (November 2022)

Call to Action

Hello,

I am Dr. Shawn Morrow, Assistant Professor of Political Science, Security Studies, & Criminal Justice. Public Policy of Administration, Terrorism, Mediation, Peace, & Criminology are areas of my expertise. My previous research on Voter Turnout, Voter Demographics in Texas as well as Fake Social and News Media effects on Law Enforcement have been downloaded more than 7500 times and cited in several articles and books. I enjoy working and consulting research projects from many different topics. I would love to help you publish and/or research your next publication.

For consultations or assistance with research please contact me at:

Email: professorshawnmorrow@gmail.com